Return to Poland

The Collected Speeches of John Paul II

COLLINS

Published by Collins

London   Glasgow   Cleveland   New York
Toronto   Sydney   Auckland   Johannesburg

First published in Great Britain, 1979
UK ISBN 0 00 215382 3

First published in the USA, 1979
Library of Congress Catalog Card Number 79–54150
USA ISBN 0–529–05710–7

Made and printed in Italy by Casa Editrice Marietti, Torino

Return to Poland

Introduction

by VALERIO VOLPINI
Editor of *L'Osservatore Romano*

The Pope went to Poland at the invitation of the Polish hierarchy and the journey was intended to have, and did indeed have, the character of a pilgrimage to his native land in the year commemorating the ninth centenary of the martyrdom of St Stanislaus, Bishop of Cracow.

A pilgrimage is a Christian feast. It is a prayer, a communion with fellow Christians. The pilgrimage of John Paul II, chosen by Christ as his own vicar, was first and foremost a pastoral action to show forth the presence of the Church's faith, ever renewed and always living in the world; that faith which it is part of the Pope's mission to sustain and to fortify.

This pilgrimage, however, also included a number of human and spiritual elements which I should like to mention. The Polish Pope was returning home for nine days, back to the distant country from which the power of the Holy Spirit had abducted him to make him a universal Pastor. Before he left, we thought of his joy in seeing his homeland again, *his* first diocese, *his* fellow Poles. We recalled the bright October evening last year when his name was proclaimed from the loggia of St Peter's; when, in the general rejoicing at our having the new Pope among us, we failed to realize that in addition to his burden of guiding the Church, he would have to endure the weight of separation both from his native land and from the communities where for so long he had been a friend, a brother, a pastor; in a word, that he would now suffer the pain of exile.

When boarding the plane which carried him to Warsaw, we imagined that he must be the most anxious and deeply affected among us all. We thought of the emotions which must be stirring in his heart and of the vivid memories conjured up in his mind. Thinking thus, it did not seem to us that we were being indiscreet, even though we may have been so, but rather we believed that we were participating more fully in the pilgrimage which was now about to begin. It appeared to us natural to attribute to the Pope (who from the beginning of his reign by word and by action had emphasized the individuality and uniqueness of each human being) this special joy, and to share it with him to the fullest extent. For is this not a part of the Christian syntony, the interior concord between the Popes and the faithful, the Christian harmony among brothers and sons? We were able also, in this way, to become aware of the great burden which the Pope has to carry entirely alone, and to show at least a small measure of gratitude for what he has given, and continues to give us.

What we could never have guessed was the depth of feeling which the pilgrimage aroused, a feeling very different, however, from what is referred to as mass or popular enthusiasm. The attraction exercised by the Pope, by his presence, in his meetings, at the celebration of the Mass, reciting prayers, singing songs; the dialogue with his brethren of every place, condition and age, was living proof of the faith of a people and became an example of what is, visibly, the unity in love of the whole Church. The nine days were like a great, and always moving, embrace in the reciprocal charity of Christ, symbolized by the Pope's kissing Polish soil when he landed in Warsaw and when he left the airport at Cracow. To have witnessed in the successor of Peter and in the People of God such expressions of brotherhood, joy, affection, and sometimes of sorrow, was to grasp the meaning of the great commandment 'that you love one another as I have loved you'.

No doubt this journey of John Paul II will be talked of and written about for a long time to come and his words will be read and pondered, but nobody can measure the spiritual impact of this pilgrimage in the hearts of men. That is part of the secret and mysterious history of the Church. It is a question of a supernatural balance which cannot be weighed by mundane rules. In any case the Church never attempts to strike such a balance; it seeks to carry into effect its covenant with Christ to maintain and stimulate the faith relying on his promise to remain with us always.

The commemoration of the ninth centenary of the martyrdom of St Stanislaus, was celebrated by an ecclesial community which, though sorely tried by human circumstances, has remained so thriving and vigorous that it is a witness for Christ in our times as it had been in other periods.

Those who accompanied the Pope on his crowded tour to Warsaw,

Gniezno, Czestochowa in the Sanctuary of Jasna Góra, Cracow, Kalwaria, Wadowice, Oswiecim (Auschwitz), Brzezinka, Nowy Targ, Mogila (Nowa Huta) in the Sanctuary of the Holy Cross – whoever followed the Pope's itinerary in all these places, must have received the most vivid impression of a Poland *semper fidelis*. Clearly, all the Poles wanted to be with him during these days and to talk to him, demonstrating the strength of their loyalty by waiting for him hour after hour, coming together in vast, well-disciplined crowds, praying while they waited to show him their love.

The portrayal of this tour which the world was able to obtain from its coverage by television, radio or in the press, even when it was most ample and objective, could scarcely have provided a real picture of the Pope's meeting with the faithful, for the media are unable to record the movements of the spirit. Words too are inadequate – and equally those which I am writing now – since one cannot convey the excitement of the soul, the fleeting looks exchanged, the silent suspense during the great moments of eucharistic celebration, the songs as they rise and fall. How can one describe the radiance in a smile or the fullness of tears? I must speak rather of the external symbols: the lights, the white and yellow flags; the flower arrangements. There were flowers everywhere, so many that you might imagine that all the flowers of spring had been cut as an offering of welcome to the pilgrim Pope.

The speeches and addresses by the Pope, collected in this volume constitute, as a whole, an uninterrupted dialogue because the crowds replied with words and songs, sometimes as prayer and sometimes as songs of gratefulness; and the Pope joined these vast choirs in music which at times was especially tender, sometimes grave and at other times imbued with faith and with hope. Some of these hymns were to Our Lady, and I was able to guess the words, knowing the melodies which are the same in all the Marian sanctuaries of Europe and the world.

During the days of the pilgrimage, we were able to see and to feel the compactness of brotherhood in this wonderful Polish Church, united to the

See of Peter, to its Primate, to its bishops. We understood as never before the depth of a faith which is also the spirit of a people. We also observed the promise of a new spring in so many thousands of young people, deacons, priests, religious, laymen and women — it was the young who were always there in the greatest numbers as if to confirm the ferment within the Polish Church and as a sign for the future. 'You are the hope of the Church', the Pope told them. Their future will assuredly be worthy of the present, just as the present has its roots deep in the past.

The Pope has brought back from Poland a great spiritual gift, which is also a symbol of something already stirring in many other Church communities throughout the world. There is in the Church an osmosis which, by prayer and good works, operates through God's power in what one might call the law of the communicating cells of the spirit; for ever living and youthful in its completeness, it assists the growth of the universal Church. Prayer has no need of the amplifier repeaters used by the mass media, in order to reach God and flow out upon the brethren; it penetrates into all the fissures and the sufferings of mankind; it rekindles hope and love.

The Pope, who in the Victory Square in Warsaw recalled the horrors of the war; who went to Auschwitz to pray in the dreadful cell where Father Kolbe sanctified the love of one's neighbour in a place planned in hatred; the Pope who celebrated Mass behind the wire of Birkenau (how these names evoke the long night of terror and death!) showed by his actions, which were so attuned to the tragic reality of our times, that only the power of love is able to defeat hatred. He proclaimed once more that to deprive men of Christ is an offence against man and a degradation of his greatness.

And so, when he returned to Rome, John Paul II brought with him the gift of an extraordinary witness to the faith; a gift of consolation for all who believe in the pre-eminence of love and peace. This gift was the response of a people, who live by their faith above all else, to the teaching and encouragement they were given throughout the nine days of the pilgrimage.

I have not mentioned in detail all the incidents of the Holy Father's journey, advisedly, but have attempted, no doubt inadequately, to describe how the Pope's words were received as they were spoken. Those who read his speeches will be able to obtain a deeper understanding of the significance of his pilgrimage; to take part in this religious happening which like all events in the life of the Church is part of a continuous and expanding history.

Like being between
two fatherlands

Saturday 2 June

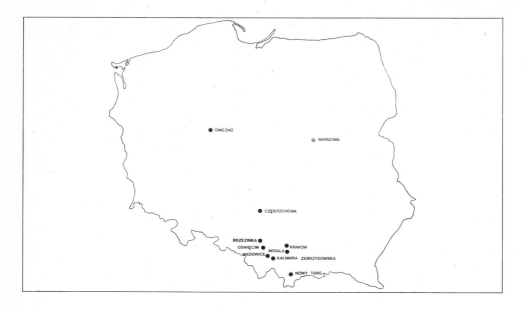

AT FIUMICINO AIRPORT

'Like being between two fatherlands.'
That was how John Paul II, speaking to
the authorities at Rome's international
airport on the morning of 2 June,
described his voyage from Italy to
Poland. It was just before he boarded
the plane which was to carry him to
Poland on his second apostolic
pilgrimage. Here is the text of his
speech:

At the moment of leaving the beloved soil of Italy to go to the beloved soil of
Poland, I have the deep impression that the journey is taking place, as it
were, between two homelands and, as if by physical contact, serves to unite
them even more in my heart. I am leaving my country of election, where the
Lord's will has called me for an exceptional pastoral service, and am going to
my country of origin, which I left just a few months ago: it is, therefore, a
return, which will shortly be followed by another return, after following an
itinerary which — like my proceeding journey in Mexico — is, by my own
choice, inspired by a religious and pastoral motivation.

It is, in fact, the recurrence of the jubilee of St Stanislaus, bishop and
martyr, that guides my steps. His sacrifice for the faith, nine centuries ago is
— like the preceding and fundamental *Millennium Poloniae* — one of the.

most important historico-religious events of my native land, so it was decided some time ago to commemorate it with appropriate and solemn celebrations. And I who had already taken part in carrying out a vast programme of spiritual preparation for the event, could not fail to be present at this appointment with my people. I am all the more grateful for the invitation of the Polish Episcopate, headed by the Primate Cardinal Stefan Wyszynski. God willing, I will first reach Warsaw, the glorious capital, so sorely tired and now risen again, industrious and pulsating with life. I will then visit Gniezno, the city which was the cradle of the Christian faith for the Polish nation, because the sovereign Mieszko was baptized there in 996, and which is distinguished by devotion to the Patron Saint Woieiech. Then the famous Marian Sanctuary of Czestochowa; and then Crakow, which with unchanged affection I continue to call 'my' city. The ancient capital of Poland, it was the episcopal see of the martyr Stanislaus, and for me close to Wadowice, the city of my youth and the field of a thirty-year apostolate. At Crakow what I would call the personal motive of this journey assumes importance, because I will meet the Church from which I come.

But there is also an international motive, and in this connection I wish to recall the kind and respectful message that has reached me from Prof. Henryk Jablonski, President of the Council of State of the People's Republic of Poland, who, also on behalf of the Polish Government, has wished to express to me the satisfaction of the whole national community at the fact that the

'son of the Polish people', called to guide the universal Church, is about to visit his homeland. This is an act which gave, and still gives me, deep pleasure. For this reason I renew my most sincere appreciation to the Authorities of the Polish State, while I confirm what I already expressed in my letter of reply: that is, my attachment to the causes of peace, coexistence and co-operation among nations; the hope that my visit will consolidate internal unity among my beloved fellow-countrymen and also serve the further development of the relations between State and Church.

It is with these sentiments and thoughts that I prepare to set off, taking with me also the good wishes of my predecessor, Paul VI. I take with me the image of all of you, Authorities and Gentlemen, who have come with such courteousness – for which I am sincerely grateful – to see me off. Above all, I take with me the bond of affection that unites me with beloved Italy and its citizens.

AT OKĘCIE AIRPORT

After a flight of a little less than two
hours, the papal plane landed safely at
10.07 on the runway of the military
airport of Okęcie near Warsaw. After
being greeted by the President of the
People's Republic of Poland, Professor
Henryk Jabloński, and by the Primate of
Poland, Cardinal Stefan Wyszyński,
John Paul II addressed the following
salutation to the authorities and to the
faithful who had come to meet him:

Mr Chairman of the Council of State of the Polish People's Republic,

1.   I express my sincere gratitude for the words with which you have greeted
me at the beginning of my stay in Poland. I thank you for what you were so
good to say with regard to the Apostolic See and myself. Through you, Mr
Chairman, I express my esteem for the State Authorities and I again renew
my cordial gratitude for the kind attitude towards my visit to Poland, 'the
beloved motherland of all Poles', my own motherland.

I desire to recall here once again the courteous letter which I received
from you last March, in which you wished, in your own name and in that of
the Government of the Polish People's Republic, to express satisfaction for the
fact that 'the son of the Polish nation called to the supreme dignity of the
Church' desired to visit his motherland. I recall these words with gratitude.
At the same time it is useful to repeat what I have already pointed out: that
is, that my visit has been dictated by strictly religious motives. Furthermore,
I earnestly hope that my present journey in Poland may serve the great cause
of *rapprochement* and of collaboration among nations; that it may be useful
for reciprocal understanding, for reconciliation, and for peace in the
contemporary world. I desire finally that the fruit of this visit may be the
internal unity of my fellow-countrymen and also a further favourable
development of the relations between the State and the Church in my beloved
motherland.

Your Eminence the Cardinal Primate of Poland,

I thank you for your words of greeting. They are particularly dear to me
both in consideration of the Person who has spoken them and on account of
the Church in Poland, whose feelings and thoughts they express.

I wish to give a response to your words by means of the whole of the
service that it is planned for me to give in the programme for the days that
Divine Providence and your cordial kindness are granting me to pass in
Poland.

Beloved brothers and sisters, dear fellow-countrymen,

2.   I have kissed the ground of Poland on which I grew up, the land from

which, through the inscrutable design of Providence, God called me to the Chair of Peter in Rome, the land to which I am coming today as a pilgrim.

I would like therefore to address you and greet each and every one of you with the same words I used on 16 October last year to greet those present in Saint Peter's Square: Praised be Jesus Christ!

3.   I greet you in the name of Christ, as I learned to greet people here in Poland.
    — in Poland, my native land, to which I remain deeply attached by the roots of my life, of my heart, of my vocation;
    — in Poland, this country in which, as the poet Cyprian Norwid wrote, 'people gather up, through respect for heaven's gifts, every crumb that falls to the ground'; where the first greeting is an eternal confession of Christ: Praised be Jesus Christ!
    — in Poland, whose thousand years of history makes it part of Europe and of contemporary humanity;
    — in Poland, which throughout the course of history has been linked with the Church of Christ and the See of Rome by a special bond of spiritual unity.

4.   Beloved brothers and sisters,
    fellow-countrymen,

I am coming to you as a son of this land, of this nation, and also, by the inscrutable designs of Providence, as a Successor of Saint Peter in the See of Rome.

I thank you for not having forgotten me and for not having ceased from the day of my election to help me with your prayers and to show me also such kindly benevolence.

I thank you for inviting me. I greet in spirit and embrace with my heart every human being living in the land of Poland.

I greet moreover all the guests who have gathered here from other countries for these days, and particularly those who represent the Polish Emigrants throughout the world.

5.   What feelings arise in my heart at the music and words of the national anthem, which we have listened to a moment ago with the respect due to it!

I thank you because this Pole, coming today 'from the land of Italy to the land of Poland' (Polish National Anthem), is received on the threshold of his pilgrimage in Poland with this music and these words, in which expression has always been found for the nation's unflagging will to live — 'while we live' (Polish National Anthem).

I wish my stay in Poland to help to strengthen this unflagging will to live on the part of my fellow-countrymen in the land that is our common mother and homeland. May it be for the good of all the Poles, of all the Polish families, of the nation and of the State.

May my stay — I wish to repeat it once again — help the great cause of peace, friendship in relations between nations, and social justice.

IN WARSAW'S CATHEDRAL

The first religious ceremony carried out by the Pope in his Polish pilgrimage was the meeting with the Catholic hierarchy and people of Warsaw. They were gathered in the Cathedral of St John the Baptist, an ancient church dating from the Middle Ages, destroyed entirely during the last war and now wholly rebuilt. To the representatives of the Archdiocese, John Paul II spoke as follows:

Praised be Jesus Christ!

At the start of my pilgrimage through Poland I greet the Church of Warsaw gathered in its Cathedral. I greet the Capital and the Archdiocese.

I greet this Church in the person of its Bishop, the Primate of Poland.

Saint Ignatius of Antioch gave expression, even in that early time, to the unity that the Church attains in its Bishop. The teaching of this great apostolic Father and martyr passed into Tradition. It was echoed amply and forcefully in the Constitution *Lumen Gentium* of the Second Vatican Council.

This teaching has found a magnificent incarnation in this very place, in Warsaw, in the Church in Warsaw. For the Cardinal Primate has become a special keystone of that unity. A keystone is what forms the arch, what reflects the strength of the foundations of the building. The Cardinal Primate shows the strength of the foundation of the Church, which is Jesus Christ. This is what his strength consists of. The Cardinal Primate has been teaching for over thirty years that he owes this strength to Mary, the Mother of Christ. We all know well that it is possible, thanks to Mary, to make the strength of the foundation that is Christ shine out, and effectively to become a keystone of the Church.

This is taught by the life and ministry of the Primate of Poland.

He is the keystone of the Church of Warsaw and the keystone of all the Church of Poland. This is what constitutes the providential mission that he has been performing for more than thirty years. I wish to give expression to this at the beginning of my pilgrimage, here in the Capital of Poland, and I also desire to give thanks for it, together with all the Church and the nation, to the Most Holy Trinity. For, in all her aspects of time and space, of geography and history, the Church is gathered in the unity of the Father, of the Son and of the Spirit, as the Council too reminds us (*Lumen Gentium*, 4).

2.   So, in the name of the Most Holy Trinity, I wish to greet all those who constitute this Church in communion with their Bishop, the Primate of Poland. The Bishops — the aged Bishop Wacław, Bishop Jerzy, Bishop Bronisław, Secretary of the Polish Bishops' Conference, Bishop Wladysław and Bishop Zbigniew.

The Metropolitan Chapter,

All the diocesan and regular clergy and the religious Brothers,

The Sisters of all the Congregations,

The Seminary,

The Ecclesiastical Academic Institution that is the continuation of the Theology Faculty of the University of Warsaw.

I wish also, in union with the Archbishop of the Church of Warsaw, to see and embrace in the fullest way the whole of the community of the People of God represented by almost three million laypeople.

The Church is present 'in the world' through the laity. I wish therefore to embrace all of you who constitute the pilgrim Church on earth, in the land of Poland, in Warsaw, in Mazowsze.

Fathers and Mothers. You who are lonely. Young People and Children. You who are old.

All of you who work on the land, in industry, in offices, in schools, in universities, in hospitals, in cultural institutes, in the ministries, everywhere. Members of all the professions who by your work are building the Poland of today, the heritage of so many generations, a well-loved heritage, a difficult heritage, a great commitment, our 'great community duty' as Poles, the Motherland (C. K. Norwid).

All of you who are at the same time the Church, this Church of Warsaw. You who are confirming the thousand-year-old right of citizenship that this Church has in the present-day of the Capital, of the nation, of the State.

3.   In union with the Church of the Archdiocese I also greet all the Bishops who are suffragans of the Metropolitan of Warsaw: the Ordinaries of Łodz, of Sandomierz, of Lublin, of Siedlce, of Warmia and of Płock, with their Auxiliary Bishops and those who have come to represent the Dioceses.

4.   The Cathedral of Warsaw, dedicated to Saint John the Baptist, was almost completely destroyed during the Rising. The one we are now in is a completely new building. It is also a sign of new Polish and Catholic life, having its centre in the Cathedral. It is a sign of what Christ once said: 'Destroy this temple, and in three days I will raise it up' (Jn 2:19).

Beloved brothers and sisters.

Dear fellow-countrymen.

You know that I am coming here to Poland for the ninth centenary of the martyrdom on Saint Stanislaus. He is the principal Patron of the Archdiocese of Warsaw. I am therefore beginning my veneration of him here, in Warsaw, at the first stopping place in my jubilee pilgrimage.

He once occupied the bishopric of Cracow, which for centuries was the capital of Poland, and it seems that he once said of himself to King Bolesław: 'Destroy this Church, and Christ, over the generations, will rebuild it'. 'He spoke of the temple of his body' (Jn 2:21).

Within this sign of the new building and the new life that is Christ and belongs to Christ, I am today meeting you, dearly beloved, and I greet you as the first Pope from the Polish race, on the threshold of the second Millenium of the Nation's Baptism and history.

'Christ . . . will never die again; death no longer has dominion over him' (Rom 6:9).

THE MEETING WITH THE CIVIL AUTHORITIES

The Holy Father met the principal state authorities, during the early afternoon of 2 June, in the Belvedere Palace which is the government's official residence. To them he addressed the following speech:

Gentlemen, Mr First Secretary,

1. 'A Poland that is prosperous and serene is also beneficial for tranquillity and good collaboration among peoples of Europe.' I take the liberty of beginning with these words pronounced by the unforgettable Paul VI in his response to the Discourse of the First Secretary, during the meeting in the Vatican on 1 December 1977 (cf. *L'Osservatore Romano*, 2 December 1977). I am convinced that these words constitute the best motto for my response today to his Discourse, which we have all listened to with the deepest attention. Nevertheless, in this my response, I wish first of all to express my gratitude for such kind words addressed both to the Apostolic See and to me. I add a word of thanks to the Authorities of the State of the Polish People's Republic for their kind attitude in regard to the invitation of the Polish Episcopate, which expresses the will of the Catholic society in our motherland, and which on their part have also opened to me the gates of my native land. I renew this gratitude and at the same time I extend it, keeping in mind all that of which I have become the debtor to the various bodies of the central and local Authorities, in view of their contribution to the preparation and actuation of this visit.

2. Passing along the streets of Warsaw, which are so dear to the heart of every Pole, I could not restrain my emotion in thinking of the great but also sad historic route that this city has completed in the service and also in the history of our nation. The particular links of this route constitute the Belvedere Palace and above all the royal Castle which is under reconstruction. The latter has a truly particular eloquence. In it there speak centuries of the history of the motherland, from the time the Capital of the State was transferred from Cracow to Warsaw. Centuries particularly difficult and particularly responsible. I desire to express my joy, indeed I wish to express thanks for everything and for what the castle represents. Like almost all of Warsaw it was reduced to ruins during the Rising, and it is now being rapidly reconstructed as a symbol of the State and of the sovereignty of the motherland.

We Poles feel in a particularly deep way the fact that the *raison d'être* of the State is the sovereignty of society, of the nation, of the motherland. We have learned this during the whole course of our history, and especially through the hard trials of recent centuries. We can never forget that terrible historical lesson — the loss of the independence of Poland from the end of the eighteenth century until the beginning of the twentieth. This painful and essentially negative experience has become as it were a new forge of Polish patriotism. For us, the word 'motherland' has a meaning, both for the mind and for the heart, such as the other nations of Europe and the world appear not to know, especially those nations that have not experienced, as ours has, historical wrongs, injustices and menaces. And thus the last World War and the Occupation, which Poland lived, were still for our generation such a great shock thirty-five years ago when this war finished on all fronts. At this moment there began the new period of the history of our motherland. We cannot however forget everything that influenced the experiences of the war and of the Occupation. We cannot forget the sacrifice of the lives of so many men and women of Poland. Neither can we forget the heroism of the Polish soldier who fought on all fronts of the world 'for our freedom and for yours'.

We have respect for and we are grateful for every help that we received from others at that time, while we think with sadness of the disappointments that we were not spared.

3. In the telegrams and letters which the supreme State Authorities of Poland were good enough to send me, both on the occasion of the inauguration of the Pontificate and in connection with the present invitation, there repeatedly appeared the thought of peace, coexistence, and of the drawing together of the nations in the modern world. Certainly, the desire expressed in this thought has a profound ethical meaning. Behind which there also stands the history of Polish science, beginning with Pawel Wlodkowic. Peace and the drawing together of the peoples can be achieved only on the principal of respect for the objective rights of the nation, such as: the right to existence, to freedom, to be a social and political subject, and also to the formation of its own culture and civilization.

Once again I take the liberty of repeating the words of Paul VI who, in the unforgettable meeting of 1 December 1977, expressed himself in these terms: '. . . We shall never grow tired of striving further and always as our possibilities permit us, so that conflicts between nations may be prevented or resolved with equity, and so that there may be ensured and ameliorated the indispensable bases for a peaceful living together among countries and continents. And not last of all, a more just world economic order; the abandonment of the arms race, which is ever more threatening also in the nuclear sector, as a preparation for a gradual and balanced disarmament; the development of better economic, cultural and human relations among individuals, peoples and associated groups' (L'Osservatore Romano, 2 December 1977, p. 2).

In these words there is expressed the social doctrine of the Church, which always supports authentic progress and the peaceful development of humanity. Therefore, while all forms of political, economic or cultural colonialism remain in contradiction to the exigencies of the international order, it is necessary to esteem all the alliances and pacts which are based on reciprocal respect and on the recognition of the good of every nation and of every State in the system of reciprocal relations. It is important that the nations and the States uniting themselves for the aim of a voluntary collaboration and one that is in conformity with the goal find at the same time in this collaboration the increase of their own well-being and their own prosperity. It is precisely this system of international relations and such resolutions among the States that the Apostolic See hopes for in the name of the fundamental premises of justice and peace in the contemporary world.

4.   The Church wishes to serve people also in the temporal dimension of their life and existence. Given the fact that this dimension is realized through people's membership of the various communities — national and State, and therefore at the same time social, political, economic and cultural — the Church continually rediscovers her own mission in relationship to these sectors of human life and activity. This is confirmed by the teaching of the Second Vatican Council and of the recent Popes.

By establishing a religious relationship with people, the Church consolidates them in their natural social bonds. The history of the Church in Poland has confirmed in an eminent way that the Church in our motherland has always sought, in various ways, to train sons and daughters who are of assistance to the State, good citizens, and useful and creative workers in the various spheres of social, professional and cultural life. And this derives from the fundamental mission of the Church, which everywhere and always strives to make people better, more conscious of their dignity, and more devoted in their lives to their family, social, professional and patriotic commitments. It is her mission to make people more confident, more courageous, conscious of their rights and duties, socially responsible, creative and useful.

For this activity the Church does not desire privileges, but only and exclusively what is essential for the accomplishment of her mission. And it is this direction that orientates the activity of the Episcopate, which has now been led for more than thirty years by a man of rare quality, Cardinal Stefan Wyszynski, Primate of Poland. In seeking, in this field, an agreement with the State Authorities, the Apostolic See is aware that, over and above reasons connected with creating the conditions for the Church's all-round activity, such an agreement corresponds to historical reasons of the nation, whose sons and daughters, in the vast majority, are the sons and daughters of the Catholic Church. In the light of these undoubted premises, we see such an agreement as one of the elements in the ethical and international order in Europe and the modern world, an order that flows from respect for the rights of the nation and for human rights. I therefore permit myself to express the opinion that one cannot desist from efforts and research in this direction.

5.   I also permit myself to express my happiness for all the good things that are shared in by my fellow-countrymen, living in the motherland, of whatever nature these good things may be and whatever be the inspiration from which they come. The thought that creates what is truly good must carry a sign of truth.

This good, and every further success in the greatest abundance and in every sector of life, I wish for Poland. Gentlemen, permit me to continue to consider this good as my own, and to feel my sharing in it as deeply as if I still lived in this land and were still a citizen of this State.

And with the same, or perhaps even with increased intensity by reason of distance, I shall continue to feel in my heart everything that could threaten Poland, that could hurt her, that could be to her disadvantage, that could signify stagnation or a crisis.

Permit me to continue to feel, to think and to hope thus, and to pray for this.

It is a son of the same motherland that is speaking to you.

Particularly near to my heart is everything in which solicitude is expressed for the good and for the consolidation of the family and for the moral health of the young generation.

Gentlemen,
Mr First Secretary,

I desire at the end to renew once again my cordial thanks to you and to express my esteem for all your solicitude that has as its aim the common good of fellow-citizens and the adequate importance of Poland in international life. I add the expression of my regard for all of you, the distinguished representatives of the Authorities, and for each one in particular, according to the office which you exercise and according to the dignity which you hold, as also according to the important part of responsibility that is incumbent on each one of you before history and before your conscience.

THE HOMILY IN VICTORY SQUARE IN WARSAW

The highlight of the Pope's meeting with the Poles of Warsaw was the ceremony in Victory Square on the Saturday afternoon. John Paul II said Mass in the presence of a large crowd of several hundreds of thousands of the faithful. In his homily, which was frequently interrupted by prolonged applause, the Pope reiterated his teaching on the presence of Christ in the history of nations and of men. The following is the text of his sermon:

Beloved fellow-countrymen, Dear brothers and sisters,
Participants in the Eucharistic Sacrifice celebrated today in Victory Square in Warsaw,

1.   Together with you I wish to sing a hymn of praise to Divine Providence, which enables me to be here as a pilgrim.

We know that the recently deceased Paul VI, the first pilgrim Pope after so many centuries, ardently desired to set foot on the soil of Poland, especially at Jasna Góra (the Bright Mountain). To the end of his life he kept this desire in his heart, and with it he went to the grave. And we feel that this desire — a desire so potent and so deeply rooted that it goes beyond the span of a pontificate — is being realized today in a way that it would have been difficult to foresee. And so we thank Divine Providence for having given Paul VI so strong a desire. We thank it for the pattern of the pilgrim Pope that he began with the Second Vatican Council. At a time when the whole Church has become newly aware of being the People of God, a People sharing in the mission of Christ, a People that goes through history with that mission, a 'pilgrim' People, the Pope could no longer remain a 'prisoner of the Vatican'. He had to become again the pilgrim Peter, like the first Peter, who from Jerusalem, through Antioch, reached Rome to give witness there to Christ and seal his witness with his blood.

Today it is granted to me to fulfil this desire of the deceased Pope Paul VI in the midst of you, beloved sons and daughters of my motherland. When, after the death of Paul VI and the brief pontificate of my immediate predecessor John Paul I, which lasted only a few weeks, I was, through the inscrutable designs of Divine Providence, called by the votes of the Cardinals from the chair of Saint Stanislaus in Cracow to that of Saint Peter in Rome, I immediately understood that it was for me to fulfil that desire, the desire that Paul VI had been unable to carry out at the Millennium of the Baptism of Poland.

My pilgrimage to my motherland in the year in which the Church in Poland is celebrating the ninth centenary of the death of Saint Stanislaus is surely a special sign of the pilgrimage that we Poles are making down through the history of the Church not only along the ways of our motherland but also along those of Europe and the world. Leaving myself aside at this point, I must nonetheless with all of you ask myself why, precisely in 1978, after so many centuries of a well established tradition in this field, a son of the Polish Nation, of the land of Poland, was called to the chair of Saint Peter. Christ demanded of Peter and of the other Apostles that they should be his 'witnesses in Jerusalem and in all Judea and Samaria and to the end of the earth' (Acts 1:8). Have we not the right, with reference to these words of Christ, to think that Poland has become nowadays the land of a particularly responsible witness? The right to think that from here – from Warsaw, and also from Gniezno, from Jasna Góra, from Cracow and from the whole of this historic route that I have so often in my life traversed and that it is right that I should traverse it again during these days – it is necessary to proclaim Christ with singular humility but also with conviction? The right to think that one must come to this very place, to this land, on this route, to read again the witness of his Cross and his Resurrection? But if we accept all that I have dared to affirm in this moment, how many great duties and obligations arise? Are we capable of them?

2.   Today, at the first stopping place in my papal pilgrimage in Poland, it is granted to me to celebrate the Eucharistic Sacrifice in Victory Square in Warsaw. The liturgy of the evening of Saturday the Vigil of Pentecost takes us to the Upper Room in Jerusalem, where the Apostles, gathered around Mary the Mother of Christ, were on the following day to receive the Holy Spirit. They were to receive the Spirit obtained for them by Christ through the Cross, in order that through the power of this Spirit they might fulfil his command: 'Go therefore and make disciples of all nations, baptizing them in the name of the Father and of the Son and of the Holy Spirit, teaching them to observe all that I commanded you (Mt 28:19–20). Before Christ the Lord left the world, he transmitted to the Apostles with these words his last recommendation, his 'missionary mandate'. And he added: 'Lo, I am with you always, to the close of the age' (Mt 28:20).

It is good that my pilgrimage to Poland on the ninth centenary of the martyrdom of Saint Stanislaus should fall in the Pentecost period and on the solemnity of the Most Holy Trinity. Fulfilling the desire of Paul VI after his death, I am able to relive the Millennium of the Baptism on Polish soil and to inscribe this year's jubilee of Saint Stanislaus in the Millennium since the beginning of the nation and the Church. The Solemnity of Pentecost and that of the Most Holy Trinity bring us close to this beginning. In the apostles who receive the Holy Spirit on the day of Pentecost are spiritually present in a way all their successors, all the Bishops, including those whose task it has been for a thousand years to proclaim the Gospel on Polish soil. Among them was this Stanislaus of Szczepanów, who paid with his blood for his mission on the episcopal chair of Cracow nine centuries ago.

On the day of Pentecost there were gathered, in the Apostles and around them, not only the representatives of the peoples and tongues listed in the book of the Acts of the Apostles. Even then there were gathered about them the various peoples and nations that, through the light of the Gospel and the

power of the Holy Spirit, were to enter the Church at different periods and centuries. The day of Pentecost is the birthday of the faith and of the Church in our land of Poland also. It is the proclamation of the mighty works of God in our Polish language also. It is the beginning of Christianity in the life of our nation also, in its history, its culture, its trials.

3a. To Poland the Church brought Christ, the key to understanding that great and fundamental reality that is man. For man cannot be fully understood without Christ. Or rather, man is incapable of understanding himself fully without Christ. He cannot understand who he is, nor what his true dignity is, nor what his vocation is, nor what his final end is. He cannot understand any of this without Christ.

Therefore Christ cannot be kept out of the history of man in any part of the globe, at any longitude or latitude of geography. The exclusion of Christ from the history of man is an act against man. Without Christ it is impossible to understand the history of Poland, especially the history of the people who have passed or are passing through this land. The history of people. The history of the nation is above all the history of people. And the history of each person unfolds in Jesus Christ. In him it becomes the history of salvation.

The history of the nation deserves to be adequately appraised in the light of its contribution to the development of man and humanity, to intellect, heart and conscience. This is the deepest stream of culture. It is culture's firmest support, its core, its strength. It is impossible without Christ to understand and appraise the contribution of the Polish nation to the development of man and his humanity in the past and its contribution today also: 'This old oak tree has grown in such a way and has not been knocked down by any wind since its root is Christ' (Piotr Skarga, *Kazania Sejmove* IV, Biblioteka Narodowa, I, 70, p. 92). It is necessary to follow the traces of what, or rather who, Christ was for the sons and daughters of this land down the generations. Not only for those who openly believed in him and professed him with the faith of the Church, but also for those who appeared to be at a distance, outside the Church. For those who doubted or were opposed.

3b. It is right to understand the history of the nation through man, each human being of this nation. At the same time man cannot be understood apart from this community that is constituted by the nation. Of course it is not the only community, but it is a special community, perhaps that most intimately linked with the family, the most important for the spiritual history of man. It is therefore impossible without Christ to understand the history of the Polish nation – this great thousand-year-old community – that is so profoundly decisive for me and each one of us. If we reject this key to understanding our nation, we lay ourselves open to a substantial misunderstanding. We no longer understand ourselves. It is impossible without Christ to understand this nation with its past so full of splendour and also of terrible difficulties. It is impossible to understand this city, Warsaw, the capital of Poland, that undertook in 1944 an unequal battle against the aggressor, a battle in which it was abandoned by the allied powers, a battle in which it was buried under its own ruins – if it is not remembered that under those same ruins there was also the statue of Christ the Saviour with his cross that is in front of the church at Krakowskie Przedmiéscie. It is impossible to understand the history of Poland from Stanislaus in Skalka to Maximilian Kolbe at Oswiecim unless we apply to them that same single fundamental criterion that is called Jesus Christ.

The Millennium of the Baptism of Poland, of which Saint Stanislaus is the first mature fruit – the millennium of Christ in our yesterday and today – is the chief reason for my pilgrimage, for my prayer of thanksgiving together with all of you, dear fellow-countrymen, to whom Christ does not cease to teach the great cause to man; together with you, for whom Jesus Christ does not cease to be an ever open book on man, his dignity and his rights and also a book of knowledge on the dignity and rights of the nation.

Today, here in Victory Square, in the capital of Poland, I am asking with all of you, through the great Eucharistic prayer, that Christ will not cease to be for us an open book of life for the future, for our Polish future.

4.   We are before the tomb of the Unknown Soldier. In the ancient and contemporary history of Poland this tomb has a special basis, a special reason for its existence. In how many places in our native land has that soldier fallen! In how many places in Europe and the world has he cried with his death that there can be no just Europe without the independence of Poland marked on its map! On how many battlefields has that soldier given witness to the rights of man, indelibly inscribed in the inviolable rights of the people, by falling for 'our freedom and yours'!

'Where are their tombs, O Poland? Where are they not! You know better than anyone – and God knows it in heaven' (A. Oppman, *Pacierz za zmarłych*).

The history of the motherland written through the tomb of an Unknown Soldier!

I wish to kneel before this tomb to venerate every seed that falls into the earth and dies and thus bears fruit. It may be the seed of the blood of a soldier shed on the battlefield, or the sacrifice of martyrdom in concentration camps or in prisons. It may be the seed of hard daily toil, with the sweat of one's brow, in the fields, the workshop, the mine, the foundries and the factories. It may be the seed of the love of parents who do not refuse to give life to a new human being and undertake the whole of the task of bringing him up. It may be the seed of creative work in the universities, the higher institutes, the libraries and the places where the national culture is built. It may be the seed of prayer, of service of the sick, the suffering, the abandoned – 'all that of which Poland is made'.

All that in the hands of the Mother of God – at the foot of the cross on Calvary and in the Upper Room of Pentecost!

All that – the history of the motherland shaped for a thousand years by the succession of the generations (among them the present generation and the coming generation) and by each son and daughter of the motherland, even if they are anonymous and unknown like the Soldier before whose tomb we are now.

All that — including the history of the peoples that have lived with us and among us, such as those who died in their hundreds of thousands within the walls of the Warsaw ghetto.

All that I embrace in thought and in my heart during this Eucharist and I include it in this unique most holy Sacrifice of Christ, on Victory Square.

And I cry — I who am a Son of the land of Poland and who am also Pope John Paul II — I cry from all the depths of this Millennium, I cry on the vigil of Pentecost:

Let your Spirit descend.
Let your Spirit descend,
and renew the face of the earth,
the face of this land.

Amen.

With what measure
is man to be measured?

Sunday 3 June

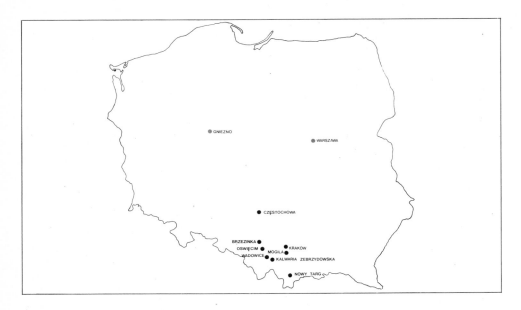

WITH THE UNIVERSITY STUDENTS OF WARSAW

'Pray for the gift of wisdom, of intelligence, of good counsel, of strength, of knowledge and piety, of human dignity and sanctification in mind and body.' These words were addressed by John Paul II to some hundreds of thousands of young university students who had spent the night in prayer in the Church of St Anne, and in the square in front of it, and who then heard Mass, on Sunday 3 June, in the presence of the Pope. He preached the following sermon:

My very dear friends,

1.   It is my ardent desire that today's meeting, which is marked by the presence of the university students, will be in keeping with the grandeur of the day and its liturgy.

The university students of Warsaw and those of the other seats of learning in this central metropolitan region are the heirs of specific traditions going back through the generations to the mediaeval 'scholars' connected principally with the Jagellonian University, the oldest university in Poland. Today every large city in Poland has its university. Warsaw has several. They bring together hundreds of thousands of students who are being trained in various branches of knowledge and are preparing for intellectual professions and particularly important tasks in the life of the nation.

I wish to greet all of you who have gathered here. I wish also to greet in you and through you all the university and academic world of Poland: all the higher institutes, the professors, the researchers, the students. I see in you, in a certain sense, my younger colleagues, because I too owe to the Polish university the basis of my intellectual formation. I had a systematic connection with the lecture halls of the faculty of philosophy and theology at Cracow and Lublin. Pastoral care of those in the universities is something for which I have had a particular liking. I therefore wish on this occasion to greet also all those who dedicate themselves to this pastoral care, the groups of the spiritual assistants of university students, and the Polish Episcopate's Commission for University Pastoral Care.

2. We are meeting today on the Solemnity of Pentecost. With the eyes of our faith we see appear before us the upper room in Jerusalem from which the Church came forth and in which the Church remains for ever. There it was that the Church was born as the living community of the People of God, as a community aware of its own mission in the history of man.

Today the Church prays: 'Come, Holy Spirit, fill the hearts of your faithful and enkindle in them the fire of your love' (Liturgy of Pentecost). These words, so often repeated, today resound with particular ardour.

Fill the hearts.

Consider, young friends, how great is the human heart, if God alone can fill it with the Holy Spirit.

Through your university studies you see open up before you the wonderful world of human knowledge in its many branches. Step by step with this knowledge your self-awareness is certainly developing also. Assuredly you have long been putting the question to yourselves: 'Who am I?' This is, I would say, the most interesting question. The fundamental query. What is to be the measurement for measuring man? That of the physical forces at his command? That of the senses that enable him to have contact with the external world? Or that of the intelligence obtained by means of the various tests or examinations?

Today's answer, the answer of the liturgy of Pentecost, points to two measurements: Man must be measured by the measurement of his 'heart' . . . In biblical language the heart means the inner spirituality of man; in particular it means conscience . . . Man must therefore be measured by the measurement of conscience, by the measurement of the spirit open to God. Only the Holy Spirit can 'fill' this heart, that is to say, lead it to self-realization through love and wisdom.

3. Therefore let this meeting with you today in front of the upper room of our history, the history of the Church and of the nation, be above all a prayer to obtain the gifts of the Holy Spirit.

As once my father placed a little book in my hand and pointed out to me the prayer to receive the gifts of the Holy Spirit, so today I, who am also called 'Father' by you, wish to pray with the university students of Warsaw and of Poland:

— for the gift of wisdom, understanding, counsel, fortitude, knowledge, piety (that is to say the sense of the sacred value of life, of human dignity, of the sanctity of the human body and soul) and, finally, for the gift of the fear of God, of which the Psalmist says that it is the beginning of wisdom (cf. Ps 11:10).

Receive from me this prayer that my father taught me, and remain faithful to it. You will thus stay in the upper room of the Church, united with the deepest stream of its history.

4.   Very much will depend on the measurement that each one of you will choose to use for your own life and your own humanity. You know well that there are different measurements. You know that there are many standards for appraising a human being, for judging him even during his studies and later in his professional work, his various personal contacts, etc.

Have the courage to accept the measurement that Christ gave us in the upper room of Pentecost and the upper room of our history.

Have the courage to look at your lives from a viewpoint that is close up and yet detached, accepting as truth what Saint Paul wrote in his letter to the Romans: 'We know that the whole creation has been groaning in travail together until now' (Rom 8:22). Do we not see this suffering before our eyes? 'For the creation waits with eager longing for the revealing of the sons of God' (Rom 8:19).

Creation is waiting not only for the Universities and the various higher institutes to prepare engineers, doctors, jurists, philologists, historians, men of letters, mathematicians and technicians: it is waiting for the revealing of the sons of God. It is waiting for this revealing from you, you who in the future will be doctors, technicians, jurists, professors . . .

Try to understand that the human being whom God created in his image and after his likeness is also called in Christ, in order that in him should be revealed what is from God, in order that in each one of us God himself should to some extent be revealed.

5.   Reflect on this.

As I make my way along the route of my pilgrimage through Poland towards the tomb of Saint Wojciech (Adalbert) at Gniezno, to that of Saint Stanislaus at Cracow, to Jasna Góra — everywhere I will ask the Holy Spirit with all my heart to grant you:

such an awareness,
such a consciousness of the value and the meaning of life,
such a future for you,
such a future for Poland.

And pray for me,
that the Holy Spirit may come to the aid of our weakness.

THE ARRIVAL AT GNIEZNO BY HELICOPTER

The first encounter between the Holy
Father and the rural population of
Poland took place on Sunday 3 June in
a former military firing range prepared
as a heliport for the landing of the
helicopter which carried the Pope from
Warsaw to Gniezno. Replying to a
welcoming address from Cardinal
Wyszyński the Pope said:

Your Eminence, beloved Primate of Poland,

1. 'May God reward' the words of greeting addressed to me here, on the
way that leads to Gniezno. Here are the field and the wide meadows where
we meet to begin our pilgrimage. This pilgrimage must bring us to Gniezno,
and then from Gniezno — through Jasna Góra — to Cracow. This is like the
route of the history of the nation and also the route of our Patrons: Adalbert
and Stanislaus, united in solicitude for the Christian patrimony of this land,
next to the Mother of God at Jasna Góra.

Here, in these wide meadows I greet with veneration the nest of the
Piasts, the origin of the history of our motherland and the cradle of the
Church, in which our ancestors were united, through the bond of faith, with
the Father, with the Son, and with the Holy Spirit.

I greet this bond! I greet it with great veneration since it goes back to the
very beginning of history, and after a thousand years it continues to be intact.
And therefore I greet here, together with the illustrious Primate of Poland,
also the Metropolitan Archbishop of Poznań and the Bishops of
Szczecin-Kamien, Koszalin-Kolobrzeg, Gdansk, Pelplin and Wloclawek, with
the Auxiliary Bishops of these Sees. I greet the clergy of all the dioceses
belonging to the metropolitan community of Gniezno of the Primates. I greet
the religious families of men and women. I greet all those who have
assembled here in such great numbers. All together we are 'a chosen race, a
royal priesthood, a holy nation, a people he claims for his own' (1 Pt 2:9).
All together we form also 'the royal race of the Piasts'.

2. Dear brothers and sisters, my fellow-countrymen. I desire that my
pilgrimage through Polish land, in communion with all of you, should
become a living catechesis, the interpretation of that catechesis which entire
generations of our forebears have inscribed into our history. May this be the
catechesis of all the history of the Church and of Poland, and at the same
time the catechesis of our times.

The fundamental task of the Church is catechesis. We know this well, not
only on the basis of the work of the last Synod of Bishops, but also on the
basis of our national experiences. In the field of this work of an ever more
conscious faith that is always newly introduced into the life of each
generation, we know how much depends on the common effort of parents, of
the family, of the parish, of the priests and pastors of souls, of men and

women catechists, of the community, of the instruments of social communication, and of customs. In fact the walls of the bell towers of the churches, the crosses at the crossroads, the holy pictures on the walls of the houses — all this in a certain way, catechizes. And on this great synthesis of the catechesis of life, in the present and in the past, depends the faith of future generations.

And therefore I desire today to be with you here, in the nest of the Piasts, in this cradle of the Church — here where over a thousand years ago catechesis began on Polish soil.

And I desire to greet from here all the ecclesial communities on Polish soil, in which catechesis takes place today. All the catechetical groups in the churches, chapels, halls and rooms . . .

I desire to greet from here the young Poland, all the Polish children and all the youth gathered in those groups where they assemble perseveringly and systematically . . . Yes, I say the young Poland; and my heart turns to all the Polish children, both to those who are present here at this moment and all those who live on Polish soil.

No one of us can ever forget the following words of Jesus: 'Let the children come to me, and do not hinder them' (Lk 18:16). I want to be, before you dear Polish children, a living echo of these words of our Saviour, particularly in this year in which the Year of the Child is celebrated throughout the whole world.

With my thought and with my heart I embrace the infants that are still in the arms of their fathers and mothers. May those loving arms of parents never cease to exist! May the number be extremely small on Polish soil of those who are known as 'social' orphans, coming from broken homes or from families that are unable to educate their own children.

May all the children of pre-school age have easy access to Christ. May they be prepared with joy to receive him in the Eucharist. May they grow 'in wisdom and in stature, and in favour with God and man' (Lk 2:52), as he himself grew, in the house of Nazareth.

And as they grow up in years, as they pass from childhood to adolescence, let no one of us, dear brothers and sisters, ever be culpable in their regard, of causing that scandal of which Jesus speaks in such a severe manner. Let us meditate every once in a while on those words. May they help us to fulfil the great work of education and of catechesis with greater zeal and with a greater sense of responsibility.

3.   The Cardinal Primate has greeted me in the name of Poland always faithful. The first and fundamental proof of this fidelity, the essential condition for the future is precisely this youth, these Polish children and, at their side, their parents, the pastors of souls, the sisters, the men and women catechists, united in the daily work of catechesis throughout all the land of Poland.

May God bless all of you, just as in the past he blessed our forebears, our sovereigns Mieszko and Boleslaw, here, along the route between Poznań and Gniezno. May he bless all of you!

Accept this sign of blessing from the hands of the pilgrim Pope who is visiting you.

THE SERMON IN THE SQUARE
OUTSIDE THE CATHEDRAL AT
GNIEZNO

The Catholics of Gniezno made a great
demonstration of their affection for the
Pope when they greeted him in the
square in front of the Cathedral with a
veritable explosion of joy soon after 1
p.m. on Sunday 3 June. The Pope
celebrated Mass outside the Cathedral.
He preached the following sermon:

Your Eminence, beloved Primate of Poland,
Dear Brothers, the Archbishops and Bishops of Poland,

1.   In you I greet the whole of the People of God living in my native land —
the priests, the religious families, the laity.

I greet Poland, baptized over a thousand years ago.

I greet Poland, inserted into the mysteries of the divine life through the
sacraments of baptism and confirmation. I greet the Church in the land of my
forefathers, in hierarchical community and unity with the Successor of Saint
Peter. I greet the Church in Poland, which was guided from the beginning
by the saints, Bishops and Martyrs, Wojciech (Adalbert) and Stanislaus, in
union with the Queen of Poland, Our Lady of Jasna Góra (The Bright
Mountain — Czestochowa).

I who have come among you as a pilgrim for the great Jubilee greet all of
you, dear brothers and sisters, with the brotherly kiss of peace.

2.   Once again the day of Pentecost has come, and we are spiritually present
in the Jerusalem upper room, while at the same time we are present here in
this upper room of our Polish Millennium, in which we hear as forcefully as
ever the voice of the mystery-filled date of that beginning from which we
start to count the years of the history of our motherland and of the Church
that has been made part of it. The history of Poland ever faithful.

On the day of Pentecost, in the Jerusalem upper room, the promise is
fulfilled that was sealed with the blood of the Redeemer on Calvary: 'Receive
the Holy Spirit. If you forgive the sins of any, they are forgiven; if you retain
the sins of any, they are retained' (Jn 20:22–23). The Church is born
precisely from the power of these worlds. The Church is born of the power of
this breath. After it had been prepared during the entire life of Christ, the
Church is definitively born when the Apostles receive from Christ the gift of
Pentecost, when they receive from him the Holy Spirit. The descent of the
Spirit marks the beginning of the Church, which throughout all generations
must bring mankind — both the individuals and the nations — into the unity
of the Mystical Body of Christ. The descent of the Holy Spirit means the
beginning of this mystery and also its continuance. For the continuance is a
constant return to the beginning.

And now we hear how in the Jerusalem upper room, the Apostles were

'filled with the Holy Spirit and began to speak in other tongues, as the Spirit gave them utterance' (Act 2:4). The various languages became theirs, became their own languages, thanks to the mystery-filled action of the Holy Spirit, which 'blows where it wills' (Jn 3:8) and renews 'the face of the earth' (Ps 103/104:30).

And although the author of Acts does not list our language among those that the Apostles began to speak that day, the time would come when the Successors of the Apostles in the upper room were to begin to speak also the tongue of our forefathers and to proclaim the Gospel to the People that could understand it and receive it only in that language.

3. There is much significance in the names of the castles of the Piast dynasty in which this historic translation of the Spirit took place and in which the torch of the Gospel was lit in the land of our forefathers. The language of the Apostles resounded for the first time, as if in a new translation, in our tongue, the tongue that the people living on the banks of the Warta and the Vistula understood and that we still understand today.

The castles with which the beginning of the faith in the land of our Polish forefathers is linked are, in fact, that of Poznań — which from the earliest times, beginning two years after the baptism of Mieszko, was the residence of the Bishop — and that of Gniezno — where the great ecclesiastical and State act of the year 1000 took place: the meeting before the relics of Saint Wojciech of the envoys of Pope Silvester II of Rome with the Roman Emperor Otto III and the first Polish king (then only a prince as yet) Bolesław Chrobry (Boleslaus the Bold), the son and successor of Mieszko, in which the first Polish ecclesiastical province was set up, thus laying the foundations of the hierarchical order for the whole of the history of Poland. Within this ecclesiastical province of Gniezno we find in the year 1000 the episcopal sees of Cracow, Wrocław and Kołobrzeg, linked in a single ecclesiastical organization.

Every time we come to this place, we must see the upper room of Pentecost opened up before us again. And we must listen to the language of our forefathers, in which the proclamation of 'the mighty works of God' (Acts 2:11) began to resound.

It was also here that the Church in Poland intoned in 1966 its first Te Deum of thanksgiving for the Millennium of its baptism. As Metropolitan of Cracow, I had the good fortune to participate in that celebration. Today, as the first Pope of the Polish race, I would like to sing again with you this Te Deum of the Millennium. Inscrutable and wonderful are the decrees of the Lord that trace the ways leading from Silvester II to John Paul II in this place.

4. After so many centuries the Jerusalem upper room was again opened up and amazement fell no longer only on the peoples of Mesopotamia and Judea, Egypt and Asia, and visitors from Rome, but also on the Slav peoples and the other peoples living in this part of Europe, as they heard the apostles of Jesus Christ speaking in their tongue and telling in their language 'the mighty works of God'.

When in the course of history the first sovereign of Poland wished to introduce Christianity and unite with the See of Saint Peter, he turned above all to the related peoples and married Dobrawa, daughter of the Czech prince Boleslaus, who was a Christian and became the godmother of her husband and of all his subjects. With her, Poland received missionaries from various nations of Europe, from Ireland, Italy and Germany, such as the holy bishop and martyr Saint Bruno of Querfurt. In the memory of the Church in the land of the Bolesławs the deepest impression was made by Saint Wojciech, a son and pastor of the related Czech nation. Well known are his history during the time that he was Bishop of Prague, his pilgrimages to Rome and above all his stay at the court of Gniezno, which was to prepare him for his final missionary journey to the North. In the area of the Baltic Sea this exiled bishop, this tireless missionary, became the grain that falls into the ground and must die in order to bear much fruit (cf. Jn 12:24). The witness of martyrdom, the witness of blood, sealed in a special way the baptism received a thousand years ago by our forefathers. The martyred remains of the apostle Wojciech lie at the foundations of Christianity throughout the land of Poland.

5.   Today, in the year of the Lord 1979, on this anniversary of the descent of the Holy Spirit, as we go back to those beginnings, we cannot fail to hear also — as well as the language of our own forefathers — other Slav languages and related languages, languages in which there then began to be heard the voice of the upper room that was opened wide to history. These languages cannot fail to be heard especially by the first Slav Pope in the history of the Church. Perhaps that is why Christ has chosen him, perhaps that is why the Holy Spirit has led him — in order that he might introduce into the communion of the Church the understanding of the words and of the languages that still sound strange to the ear accustomed to the Romance, Germanic, English and Celtic tongues. Is it not Christ's will that the Holy Spirit should make the Mother Church turn, at the end of the second millenium of Christianity, with loving understanding, with special sensitivity, to those forms of human speech that are linked together by their common origin, their common etymology, and which, in spite of the well-known differences, even in way of writing, sound close and familiar one to another?

Is it not Christ's will, is it not what the Holy Spirit disposes, that this Pope, in whose heart is deeply engraved the history of his own nation from its very beginning and also the history of the brother peoples and the neighbouring peoples, should in a special way manifest and confirm in our age the presence of these peoples in the Church and their specific contribution to the history of Christianity?

Is it not the design of Providence that he should reveal the developments that have taken place here in this part of Europe in the rich architecture of the temple of the Holy Spirit?

Is it not Christ's will, is it not what the Holy Spirit disposes, that this Polish Pope, this Slav Pope, should at this precise moment manifest the spiritual unity of Christian Europe? Although there are two great traditions,

that of the West and that of the East, to which it is indebted, through both of them Christian Europe professes 'one faith, one baptism, one God and Father of us all' (Eph 4:5–6), the Father of our Lord Jesus Christ.

Yes, it is Christ's will, it is what the Holy Spirit disposes, that what I am saying should be said in this very place and at this moment, in Gniezno, in the land of the Piasts, in Poland, close to the relics of Saint Wojciech and Saint Stanislaus, before the image of the Virgin Mother of God, Our Lady of the Bright Mountain and Mother of the Church.

On the occasion of the baptism of Poland we must call to mind the Christianization of the Slavs: that of the Croats and Slovenes, among whom missionaries worked as early as about 650 and largely accomplished their evangelization by the year 800; that of the Bulgarians, whose prince, Borys I, received baptism in 864 or 865; that of the Moravians and Slovaks, who were reached by missionaries before 850 and then in 863 by Saint Cyril and Saint Methodius, who came to Greater Moravia to consolidate the faith of the young communities; that of the Czechs, whose Prince Borivoj was baptized by Saint Methodius. The field of the evangelizing influence of Saint Methodius and his disciples also included the Vislans and the Slavs living in Serbia. We must also remember the Christianization of the Slavs dwelling along the Elbe: Obotrits, Wielets and Lusatian Sorbs. The Christianization of Europe was completed with the baptism of Lithuania in 1386 and 1387.

Pope John Paul II, a Slav, a son of the Polish nation, feels how deeply fixed in the ground of history are the roots of his origin, how many centuries stand behind the word of the Holy Spirit proclaimed by him from Saint Peter's Vatican Hill, and here at Gniezno, from the hill of Lech, and at Cracow, from the heights of Wawel.

This Pope, who is a witness of Christ and a lover of the Cross and the Resurrection, today comes to this place to give witness to Christ, who is living in the soul of his nation, to Christ, who is living in the souls of the nations that have long since accepted him as 'the way, and the truth, and the life' (Jn 14:6). He comes here to speak before the whole Church, before Europe and the world, of those often forgotten nations and peoples. He comes here to cry 'with a loud voice'. He comes here to point out the paths that in one way or another lead back towards the Pentecost upper room, towards the Cross and Resurrection. He comes here to embrace all these peoples, together with his own nation, and to hold them close to the heart of the Church, to the heart of the Mother of the Church, in whom he has unlimited trust.

6.   Within a short time there will end here in Gniezno the visit of the sacred Icon. The image of Our Lady of Jasna Góra, the image of the Mother, expresses in a unique way her presence in the mystery of Christ and of the Church that has been living for so many centuries in the land of Poland. This image, which for more than twenty years has been visiting the individual churches, dioceses and parishes of this land, ends before long its visit to Gniezno, the ancient See of the Primates, and goes to Jasna Góra, to begin its pilgrimage in the Diocese of Czestochowa.

It is a great joy for me to be able to do this stage of my pilgrimage together with Mary and to be with her on the great historic route that I have often travelled, from Gniezno to Cracow by way of Jasna Góra, from Saint Wojciech to Saint Stanislaus by way of the 'Virgin Mother of God, whom God has filled with glory, Mary'.

The chief route of our spiritual history, the route travelled by all the Poles, whether of the West or of the East, as well as those outside their motherland in the various countries and continents.

The chief route of our spiritual history and also one of the great routes of the spiritual history of all the Slavs and one of the chief spiritual routes of the history of Europe.

In these days there will take place for the first time a pilgrimage along this route by the Pope, the Bishop of Rome, the Successor of Peter, the first among those who went forth from the Pentecost upper room in Jerusalem, singing:

> 'Lord God, how great you are,
> clothed in majesty and glory,
> wrapped in light as in a robe!

> How many are your works, O Lord!
> In wisdom you have made them all.
> The earth is full of your riches.

> You send forth your Spirit, they are created,
> and you renew the face of the earth'.
> (Ps 103/104:1–2, 24, 30)

Thus, dear fellow-countrymen, will this Pope, blood of your blood, bone of your bone, sing with you, and with you he will exclaim:

> 'May the glory of the Lord last for ever!

> May the Lord rejoice in his works!

> May the glory of the Lord last for ever!

> May my thoughts be pleasing to him'.
> (Ps 103/104:31, 34)

We shall go together along this path of our history, from Jasna Góra to Wawel, to Saint Stanislaus. We shall go there, thinking of the past, but with our minds directed towards the future.

> We shall not return to the past!
> We shall go towards the future!
> 'Receive the Holy Spirit!'
> (Jn 20:22)

Amen.

THE SPEECH TO THE YOUNG PEOPLE
OF THE ARCHDIOCESE OF GNIEZNO

After spending almost the whole day
crowded into the square which lies
between the old residence of the
primate Cardinal Wyszyński and the
Cathedral dedicated to Saint Adalbert,
thousands of the faithful heard a Mass
celebrated at 5 p.m. by Cardinal
designate Wladyslaw Rubin, the
Auxiliary to the Cardinal Primate, at the
same altar at which Pope John Paul II
had himself said his second Mass since
his arrival in Poland. At the conclusion
of the Mass, John Paul II went out on to
the balcony of the Archbishop's Palace
and spoke to the crowd. He said:

Dear people,

1.   The most ancient monument of Polish literature is the *Bogurodzica*
('Mother of God'). Tradition makes its origin go back to Saint Wojciech
(Adalbert). The history of literature enables us to place in the fifteenth
century the date of the oldest texts of this song message. I call it a song
message because the *Bogurodzica* is not only a song but also a profession of
faith, a creed of Polish belief; it is a catechesis and even a document of
Christian education. The principal truths of faith and the principals of morals
are contained in it. It is not merely a historical object. It is a document of
life. Jakub-Wujek called it 'the Polish catechism'.

It is always with deep emotion, with rapture, that we sing it,
remembering that it was sung at solemn and decisive moments. We read it
with deep feeling. It is difficult to read these ancient verses in any other way,
if we think of the fact that the generation of our forefathers were brought up
on them. The song of the *Bogurodzica* is not just an ancient cultural
document. It has given Polish culture its fundamental original framework.

2.   Culture is an expression of man, a confirmation of humanity. Man creates
culture and through culture creates himself. He creates himself with the
inward effort of the spirit, of thought, will and heart. At the same time he
creates culture in communion with others. Culture is an expression of
communication, of shared thought and collaboration by human beings. It is
born of service of the common good and becomes an essential good of human
communities.

Culture is above all a common good of the nation. Polish culture is a
good on which the spiritual life of Poles rests. It distinguishes us as a nation.
It is decisive for us throughout the course of history, more decisive even than
material power. Indeed, it is more decisive than political boundaries. The
Polish nation, as is well known, passed through the hard trial of the loss of
its independence for over a hundred years. And in the midst of this trial it

preserved its own identity. It remained spiritually independent because it had its own culture. Indeed, in the period of the partitions it still greatly enriched its culture and made it deeper, since it is only by creating culture that it can keep itself in being.

3.   From its beginnings Polish culture bears very clear Christian signs. The baptism received throughout the thousand years by the generations of our fellow-countrymen not only initiated them into the mystery of the death and Resurrection of Christ, not only made them become children of God through grace, but also had a great echo in the history of thought and in artistic creativity, poetry, music, drama, the plastic arts, painting and sculpture.

It is still so today. Christian inspiration continues to be the chief source of the creativity of Polish artists. Polish culture still flows with a broad stream of inspirations that have their source in the Gospel. This contributes also to the deeply humanistic character of this culture. It makes it so deeply and authentically human, since, as Adam Mickiewicz wrote in his *Ksiegi Narodu i Pielgrzymstwa Polskiego*, 'a civilization truly worthy of man must be a Christian civilization'.

In the works of Polish culture the soul of the nation is reflected. In them lives the nation's history, a history that is a continual school of solid sincere patriotism. For this reason, that same history can make demands and uphold ideals without which it is difficult for man to believe in his own dignity and educate himself.

You are hearing these words from a man who owes his own spiritual formation from the beginning to Polish culture, to its literature, its music, its plastic arts, its theatre — to Polish history, to the Polish Christian traditions, to the Polish schools, the Polish universities.

In speaking to you young people in this way, this man wishes above all to pay the debt that he owes this marvellous spiritual heritage that began with the *Bogurodzica*. At the same time, this man wishes to appear before you today with this heritage, which is the common good of all Poles and constitutes an outstanding part of European and world culture.

And he asks you:

Remain faithful to this heritage. Make it the foundation of your formation. Be nobly proud of it. Keep this heritage and multiply it; hand it on to future generations.

> Come, Holy Spirit,
> and from heaven direct on man
> the rays of your light.
>
> Come, Father of the poor;
> come, giver of God's gifts;
> come, light of men's hearts . . . (Pentecost Sequence).

Light of young Polish consciences, come. Strengthen in them the love from which was born the first Polish song, the *Bogurodzica*, a message of faith and dignity for man in our land.

To you, O Mother of the Church,
I entrust all the problems of this
Church

Monday 4 June

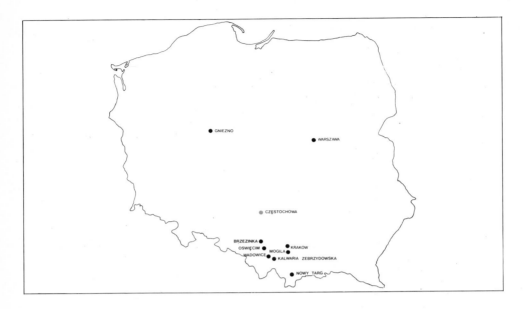

THE SERMON AT THE SANCTUARY OF THE BLACK MADONNA OF JASNA GÓRA

The Holy Father, on the morning of 4 June, presided over the concelebration of Mass at the Sanctuary of Our Lady in the monastery of Jasna Góra (Częstochowa) in an open-air ceremony attended by a vast crowd, on the esplanade behind the monastery. After the reading of the Gospel, the Pope preached the following sermon:

1. 'Holy Virgin guarding bright Czestochowa . . .'

To my mind come back these words of the poet Mickiewicz, who in an invocation to the Virgin at the beginning of his *Pan Tadeusz* expressed what then beat and still beats in the hearts of all Poles, by making use of the language of faith and that of our national tradition. It is a tradition that goes back some 600 years to the time of the blessed Queen Hedwig at the dawn of the Jagellonian dynasty. The image of Jasna Góra expresses a tradition and a language of faith still more ancient than our history and also reflecting the whole of the content of the *Bogurodzica*, on which we meditated yesterday at Gniezno, recalling the mission of Saint Wojciech (Adalbert) and going back to the first moments of the proclamation of the Gospel in the land of Poland.

She who once spoke in song, later spoke in this Image of her, manifesting through it her maternal presence in the life of the Church and of the motherland. The Virgin of Jasna Góra has revealed her maternal solicitude for every soul; for every family; for every human being living in this land, working here, fighting and falling on the battlefield, condemned to extermination, fighting against himself, winning or losing; for every human being who must leave the soil of his motherland as an emigrant; for every human being.

The Poles are accustomed to link with this place, this shrine, the many happenings of their lives: the various joyful or sad moments, especially the solemn, decisive moments, the occasions of responsibility, such as the choice of the direction for one's life, the choice of one's vocation, the birth of one's children, the final school examinations, and so many other occasions. They are accustomed to come with their problems to Jasna Góra to speak of them with their heavenly Mother, who not only has her image here, one of the best known and most venerated pictures of her in the world, but is specially present here. She is present in the mystery of Christ and of the Church, as the Council teaches. She is present for each and every one of those who come on pilgrimage to her, even if only in spirit and heart when unable to do so physically.

The Poles are accustomed to do this.

It is a custom also with related peoples, with neighbouring nations. More and more people are coming here from all over Europe and outside Europe.

During the great novena, the Cardinal Primate expressed himself as follows with regard to the significance of the shrine of Czestochowa for the life of the Church:

'What has happened at Jasna Góra?

'We are still unable to give an adequate answer. Something has happened that is beyond our powers of imagining . . . Jasna Góra has shown itself an inward bond in Polish life, a force that touches the depths of our hearts and holds the entire nation in the humble yet strong attitude of fidelity to God, to the Church and to her Hierarchy.. . . . For many of us it was a great surprise to see the power of the Queen of Poland display itself so magnificently'.

It is no wonder then that I too should come here today. I have, in fact, taken with me from Poland to the chair of Saint Peter in Rome this 'holy habit' of the heart, which has been built up by the faith of so many generations, has been tested by the Christian experience of so many centuries, and is deeply rooted in my soul.

2. Several times Pope Pius XI came here, naturally not as Pope but as Achille Ratti, the first Nuncio in Poland after the recovery of independence.

After the death of Pius XII, when Pope John XXIII was elected to the Chair of Peter, the first words of the new Pontiff to the Primate of Poland after the Conclave were a reference to Jasna Góra. He recalled his visits here during his years as Apostolic Delegate in Bulgaria and he asked above all for unceasing prayer to the Mother of God for the intentions involved in his new mission. His request was satisfied every day at Jasna Góra, not only during his pontificate but also during those of his Successors.

We all know how much Pope Paul VI wanted to come here in pilgrimage. He was so closely connected with Poland from the time of his first diplomatic appointment in the Warsaw Nunciature. He was the Pope that did so much for the normalization of the life of the Church in Poland, particularly with regard to the present arrangement of the territories in the west and the north. He was the Pope of our Millennium. It was for the Millennium that he wanted to be here as a pilgrim together with the sons and daughters of the Polish Nation.

After the Lord called Pope Paul VI to himself on the solemnity of the Transfiguration last year, the Cardinals chose his Successor on 26 August, the day in which Poland, and especially Jasna Góra, celebrates the solemnity of Our Lady of Czestochowa. The news of the election of the new Pope, John Paul I, was communicated to the faithful by the Bishop of Czestochowa in the course of the evening celebration.

What must I say of myself, to whom after the barely 33-day pontificate of John Paul I it fell on 16 October 1978 by the inscrutable decree of Providence to receive his inheritance and the apostolic succession to the Chair of Saint Peter? What must I say, I who am the first non-Italian Pope for 455 years? What must I say, I, John Paul II, the first Polish Pope in the history of the Church? I will tell you: on that 16 October, the day on which the liturgical calendar of the Church in Poland recalls Saint Hedwig, I went back

in thought to 26 August, to the preceding Conclave and the election that took place on the Solemnity of Our Lady of Jasna Góra.

I had no need even to say, as my Predecessors said, that I was going to count on the prayers offered at the foot of the image of Jasna Góra. The call of a son of the Polish nation to the Chair of Peter involves an evident strong connection with this holy place, with this shrine of great hope: so many times I had whispered *Totus tuus* in prayer before this image.

3. And today I am again with all of you, dear brothers and sisters; with you, beloved fellow-countrymen; with you, the Cardinal Primate of Poland; with all the Episcopate to which I belonged for more than twenty years as Bishop, Metropolitan Archbishop of Cracow and as Cardinal. So many times we came here to this holy place with attentive pastoral ear, to listen to the beating of the heart of the Church and of that of the motherland in the heart of the Mother. Jasna Góra is, in fact, not only a place of pilgrimage for the Poles of the motherland and of the whole world but also the nation's shrine. One must listen in this holy place in order to hear the beating of the heart of the nation in the heart of the Mother. For her heart beats, we know, together with all the appointments of history, with all the happenings in our national life: how many times, in fact, has it vibrated with the laments or the historical sufferings of Poland, but also with the shouts of joy and victory! The history of Poland can be written in different ways; especially in the case of the history of the last centuries, it can be interpreted along different lines. But if we want to know how this history is interpreted by the heart of the Poles, we must come here, we must listen to this shrine, we must hear the echo of the life of the whole nation in the heart of its Mother and Queen. And if her heart beats with a tone of disquiet, if it echoes with solicitude and the cry for the conversion and strengthening of consciences, this invitation must be accepted. It is an invitation springing from maternal love, which in its own way is shaping the historical processes in the land of Poland.

The last decades have confirmed and intensified that unity between the Polish nation and its Queen. Before the Virgin of Czestochowa there was pronounced the consecration of Poland to the Immaculate Heart of Mary on 8 September 1946. Ten years later the vows of King Jan Kazimierz were renewed at Jasna Góra on the 300th anniversary of the time when he, after a period referred to as one of deluge (the seventeenth-century Swedish invasion), proclaimed the Mother of God Queen of the Polish Kingdom. On that anniversary began the great nine-year novena in preparation for the Millennium of the Baptism of Poland. Finally, in the year of the Millennium itself, on 3 May 1966, in this place the Primate of Poland pronounced the act of total servitude to the Mother of God for the freedom of the Church in Poland and throughout the world. This historic act was pronounced here, before Paul VI, absent in body but present in spirit, as a testimony of that lively and strong faith expected and demanded by the present time.

The act speaks of 'servitude'. It contains a paradox similar to the words of the Gospel according to which one must lose one's life to find it (cf. Mt 10:39). For love constitutes the fulfilment of freedom, yet at the same time 'belonging', and so not being free is part of its essence. However, this 'not being free' in love is not felt as slavery but rather as an affirmation and fulfilment of freedom. The act of consecration in slavery indicates therefore a unique dependence and a limitless trust. In this sense slavery (non-freedom) expresses the fullness of freedom, in the same way as the Gospel speaks of the need to lose one's life in order to find it in its fullness.

The words of that act, which were spoken with the language of the historical experiences of Poland, the language of her sufferings and also of her victories, receive a response in this very moment of the life of the Church and of the world, after the close of the Second Vatican Council, which, as we rightly think, has opened a new era. The Council began an age of deeper knowledge of man, of his 'joy and hope, grief and anguish', as is stated in the first words of the Pastoral Constitution *Gaudium et Spes*. Aware of her great dignity and her magnificent vocation in Christ, the Church wishes to go to meet man. The Church wishes to respond to the eternal yet ever topical queries of human hearts and human history. For that reason she carried out during the Council a work of deeper knowledge of herself, her nature, her mission, her tasks.

On 3 May 1966 the Polish Episcopate added to this fundamental work by the Council its own act of Jasna Góra: the consecration to the Mother of God for the freedom of the Church in the world and in Poland. It was a cry coming forth from the heart and the will: a cry of the whole of the Christian being, from the person and the community, for the full right to proclaim the saving message; a cry that willed to have universal effectiveness by striking root in the present age and in the future. Everything through Mary. This is the authentic interpretation of the presence of the Mother of God in the mystery of Christ and of the Church, as is proclaimed by Chapter VIII of the Constitution *Lumen Gentium*. This interpretation corresponds to the tradition of the saints, such as Bernard of Clairvaux, Grignion de Montfort and Maximilian Kolbe.

4.   Pope Paul VI accepted this act of consecration as the fruit of the celebration of the Polish Millennium of Jasna Góra, as is shown by his bull placed close to the image of the Black Madonna of Czestochowa. Today, on coming to Jasna Góra, his unworthy Successor wishes to renew it on the day after Pentecost, the very day on which is celebrated throughout Poland the feast of the Mother of the Church.

For the first time the Pope is celebrating this solemnity, expressing together with you, Venerable and dear Brothers, his gratitude towards his great Predecessor, who from the time of the Council began to invoke Mary with the title of Mother of the Church.

This title enables us to enter into the whole of the mystery of Mary from the moment of her Immaculate Conception, passing through the Annunciation, the Visitation and the Birth of Jesus in Bethlehem, to Calvary. It enables us all to be − the scene is recalled in today's liturgy − in the upper room, where the Apostles devoted themselves to prayer, together with Mary the Mother of Jesus, as they waited, after the Lord's Ascension, for the fulfilment of his promise of the coming of the Holy Spirit, in order that the

Church might be born. A special participation in the birth of the Church is had by her to whom we owe the birth of Christ.

The Church, which was once born in the Pentecost upper room, continues to be born in every upper room of prayer. She is born to become our spiritual Mother in the likeness of the Mother of the Eternal Word. She is born to reveal the characteristics and power of that motherhood (the motherhood of the Mother of God) thanks to which we can 'be called children of God; and so we are' (1 Jn 3:1). For, in his plan of salvation, the holy fatherhood of God used the virginal motherhood of his lowly handmaiden to bring about in the children of man the work of the divine author.

Dear fellow-countrymen, venerable and beloved Brothers in the Episcopate, Pastors of the Church in Poland, illustrious guests, and all of you the faithful: consent that I, as Saint Peter's Successor present with you here today, should entrust the whole of the Church to the Mother of Christ with the same lively faith, the same heroic hope, with which we did so on the memorable day of 3 May of the Polish Millennium.

Consent that I should bring here, as I did already in the Basilica of Saint Mary Major in Rome and later in the Shrine of Guadalupe in Mexico, the mysteries of the hearts, the sorrow and suffering, and finally the hope and expectation of this final period of the twentieth century of the Christian era.

Consent that I should entrust all this to Mary.

Consent that I should entrust it to her in a new and solemn way.

I am a man of great trust.

I learnt to be so here.

Amen.

'Great Mother of God made Man, Most Holy Virgin,
Our Lady of Jasna Góra . . .'

With these words the Polish Bishops addressed you so many times at Jasna Góra, bearing in their hearts the experiences and the sufferings, the joy and the sorrow, and, above all, the faith, hope and charity of their fellow-countrymen.

May I be permitted today to begin with the same words the new act of consecration to Our Lady of Jasna Góra. This new act springs from that same faith, hope and charity, and from the tradition of our people shared by me for so many years. It springs at the same time from the new duties that, thanks to you, Mary, have been entrusted to me, an unworthy man and also your adoptive son.

How meaningful for me always have been the words that your Son, born from you, Jesus Christ, the Redeemer of man, spoke from the height of the Cross, pointing out John the Baptist: 'Woman, behold, your son!' (Jn 19:26). In these words I always found the place for every human being and the place for myself.

By the inscrutable designs of Divine Providence I am today present here at Jasna Góra, in my earthly homeland, Poland, and I wish first of all to confirm the acts of consecration and trust that at various times — 'in many and various ways' — were pronounced by the Cardinal Primate and the Polish Episcopate. In a very special way I wish to confirm and renew the act of consecration pronounced at Jasna Góra on 3 May 1966, on the occasion of the Millennium of Poland. With this act the Polish Bishops wished, by giving themselves to you, Mother of God, 'in your maternal slavery of love,' to serve the great cause of the freedom of the Church not only in their own homeland but in the whole world. Some years later, on 5 September 1971, they consecrated to you all of humanity, all the nations and peoples of the modern world, and their brothers and sisters who are close to them by faith, by language and by the destinies they share in history, extending this consecration to the furthest limits of love as is demanded by your heart, the heart of a Mother who embraces each and every person, always and everywhere.

Today I come to Jasna Góra as its first pilgrim Pope, and I wish to renew the entire heritage of trust, of consecration and of hope that has been accumulated here with such magnanimity by my Brothers in the Episcopate and my fellow-countrymen.

Therefore, I entrust to you, Mother of the Church, all the problems of this Church, the whole of her mission and of her service, while the second millennium of the history of Christianity on earth is about to draw to a close.

Spouse of the Holy Spirit and Seat of Wisdom, it is to your intercession that we owe the magnificent vision and the programme of renewal of the Church in our age that found expression in the teaching of the Second Vatican Council. Grant that we may make this vision and programme the object of our activity, our service, our teaching, our pastoral care, our apostolate — in the same truth, simplicity and fortitude with which the Holy Spirit has made them known through our humble service. Grant that the whole Church may be reborn by drawing from this fount of the knowledge of her nature and mission, and not from other foreign or poisoned 'cisterns' (cf. Jer 8:14).

Help us in the great endeavour that we are carrying out to meet in a more and more mature way our brothers in faith, with whom so many things unite us, although there is still something dividing us. Through all the means of knowledge, of mutual respect, of love, of shared collaboration in various fields, may we be able to rediscover gradually the divine plan for the unity into which we should enter and bring everybody in, in order that the one fold of Christ may recognize and live its unity on earth. Mother of unity, teach us constantly the ways that lead to unity.

Allow us in the future to go out to meet all human beings and all peoples that are seeking God and wishing to serve him on the way of different religions. Help us all to proclaim Christ and reveal 'the power of God and the wisdom of God' (1 Cor 1:24) hidden in his Cross. You were the first to reveal him at Bethlehem, not only to the simple faithful shepherds but also to the wise men from distant lands.

Mother of Good Counsel, show us always how we are to serve the individual and humanity in every nation, how we are to lead them along the ways of salvation. How we are to protect justice and peace in a world continually threatened on various sides. How greatly I desire on the occasion of our meeting today to entrust to you all the difficult problems of the societies, systems and states — problems that cannot be solved with hatred, war and self-destruction but only by peace, justice and respect for the rights of people and of nations.

Mother of the Church, grant that the Church may enjoy freedom and peace in fulfilling her saving mission and that to this end she may become mature with a new maturity of faith and inner unity. Help us to overcome opposition and difficulties. Help us to rediscover all the simplicity and dignity of the Christian vocation. Grant that there may be no lack of 'labourers in the Lord's vineyard'. Sanctify families. Watch over the souls of the young and the hearts of the children. Help us to overcome the great moral threats against the fundamental spheres of life and love. Obtain for us the grace to be continually renewed through all the beauty of witness given to the Cross and Resurrection of your Son.

How many problems should I not present to you, Mother, by name in this meeting! I entrust them all to you, because you know them best and understand them.

I entrust them to you in the place of the great consecration, from which one has a view not only of Poland but of the whole Church in the dimensions of countries and continents — the whole Church in your maternal heart.

I who am the first servant of the Church offer the whole Church to you and entrust it to you here with immense confidence, Mother. Amen.

IN THE PARISH OF SAINT SIGISMUND AT CZĘSTOCHOWA

During the afternoon, there was a meeting with the faithful of the diocese of Częstochowa to honour the miraculous painting of the Madonna of Jasna Góra. Many thousands of people were gathered in front of the Church of Saint Sigismund to see the Pope, himself a pilgrim in his native land. In speaking to them, John Paul II recalled the stages in the visitations of the pilgrim image of the Madonna of Jasna Góra.

1.   It is with real joy that I step on to the threshold of this parish which, together with the whole Diocese of Czestochowa, is awaiting the coming visit of the image of Our Lady of Jasna Góra.

After it has left the primatial See of Gniezno, it will begin its visit among you. And therefore already today I wish to greet the Mother of the visit in this new stage of her pilgrimage throughout the land of Poland. I do this in cordial spiritual union with my beloved Brother of the Diocese of Czestochowa, with the Bishops who assist him here with all the pastors and diocesan and religious priests, and with the beloved Sisters of so many religious Congregations. I do this with the heart of all God's people throughout the world who are particularly aware of the presence of Our Lady of Jasna Góra.

2.   The visit of the image of Jasna Góra, in the faithful copy of it blessed by the Holy Father Pius XII in 1957, has over twenty years of history. In the summer of 1957 the image began to visit each parish, one after another, going from the Archdiocese of Warsaw to the Diocese of Siedlce, to that of Łomza, to the Archdiocese of Białystok, to the Lake Region and Pomerania, to the Dioceses of Warmia, Gdańsk and Chelm; then to the area that was the administrature of Gorzów but is now divided into the three Dioceses of Szczecin-Kamién, Koszalin-Kołobrzeg and Gorzów, within the new boundaries. The visit of the pilgrim image next continued in Silesia – in the Archdiocese of Wrocław and the Diocese of Opole. Then it reached the Diocese of Katowice and the other southern dioceses, namely the Archdiocese of Cracow, the Dioceses of Tarnów and Przemyśl and the territory of the Archdiocese of Lubaczów, and then the Dioceses of Lublin and Sandomierz. After visiting the Diocese of Kielce, the image proceeded to the Diocese of Drohiczyn and that of Łódź, and then turned north to the Dioceses of Włocławek and Płock. From Płock the series of visits passed to the Archdiocese of Poznań and finally to that of Gniezno. Today the Diocese of Czestochowa is added, constituting as it were the last link in that magnificent chain.

I have listed all the stopping places on the visit of the pilgrim image of Our Lady of Jasna Góra, because each one of them developed the blessed idea from which the Servant of God Pope Pius XII and the Polish Episcopate drew inspiration when undertaking twenty years ago this religious practice.

3. I greeted Our Lady of Jasna Góra in her pilgrim image at various stopping places. I did so especially during its visit to the parishes and communities of the People of God in the Archdiocese of Cracow, of which I was the pastor.

Today I wish to greet her, in the inscrutable design of Providence, as the Successor of all the Popes who have lived during this period, from Pius XII to John XXIII, to Paul VI, to John Paul I. I greet Mary, thanking her for all the graces of each stage of the visit. By my personal pastoral experience I know how great and extraordinary are these graces. Through the visits of the pilgrim image of Jasna Góra, in its faithful copy, there has been as it were

the start of a new chapter in the history of Our Lady of Jasna Góra in the land of Poland.

This visit has given tangible expression to the teaching of the Second Vatican Council that is contained above all in the Dogmatic Constitution on the Church. These visits have shown what is the real maternal presence of the Mother of God in the mystery of Christ and of his Church. Going forth from her shrine of Jasna Góra to visit each diocese and each parish in Poland, Mary has shown herself to all of us in a special way as our Mother. For a mother does not merely wait at home for her children: she follows them wherever they stay. Wherever they live or work or form their families, wherever they are pinned to a bed of pain, even on whatever path they have strayed, where they are forgetful of God and weighed down by guilt.

There a mother follows her children, everywhere!

I wish therefore today, together with all of you present here, to express immense thankfulness for all of that. I wish to be the principal echo of all hearts, of all families, and communities, of all the pastors — priests and bishops. Of everybody.

At the same time, when I spiritually greet Mary in her pilgrim image at her entrance into every parish of the Diocese of Czestochowa — as the chain of the visit is passed to the Bishop of the Church of Czestochowa with his Brothers in the Episcopate, with the pastors, the priests, the religious families and all the People of God — I wish to be the messenger of a great expectation and an ardent hope. Your hearts are full of this expectation. Mary herself through her image is bringing you the hope. Was not the moment of the Annunciation in Nazareth a great turning point in the history of mankind? Did not Mary bring hope to the house of Zechariah when she went to visit her kinswoman Elizabeth? In our own difficult times did not Pope Paul VI call the Mother of God the beginning of a better world? Did not Blessed Maximilian Kolbe, the Polish 'knight' of the Immaculate, also feel the same mystery?

May Mary's stay in every parish of your Diocese of Czestochowa be blessed.

As the Servant of God Pius XII did at the beginning, so today, at the last stage of the pilgrimage of the image of Jasna Góra, I, his unworthy Successor, I, Pope John Paul II, a son of the Polish Nation, wholeheartedly bless those who welcome Mary.

I place this present greeting and blessing in the hands of the Bishop of Czestochowa, so that it may be read — as is customary — during the visit to the individual parishes.

SPEECH TO A GROUP OF INVALIDS

The allocutions by the Holy Father to
the faithful who gathered at the
Sanctuary of Jasna Góra were
continued that night when soon after
8.30 p.m., on leaving the monastery, the
Pope observed a group of invalids
among the crowd. He addressed them
as follows:

My pilgrimage to Poland cannot go without a word to the sick, who are
so close to my heart. I know, my dear friends, how in your letters to me you
often write that you are offering for my intentions the heavy cross of your
illness and suffering, that you are offering it for my mission as Pope. May the
Lord reward you.

Every time I recite the morning, midday and evening Angelus, I feel,
dear fellow-countrymen, your special closeness to me. I unite myself
spiritually with all of you. In a particular way I renew the spiritual unity that
binds me to every person who is suffering, to every one who is sick, to
everyone confined to a hospital bed, to every invalid tied to a wheelchair, to
every person who in one way or other is meeting his cross.

Dear brothers and sisters, every contact with you, no matter where it has
taken place in the past or takes place today, has been a source of deep
spiritual emotion for me. I have always felt how insufficient were the words
that I could speak to you and with which I could express my human
compassion. I have the same impression today also. I feel the same way
always. But there remains the one dimension, the one reality in which human
suffering is essentially transformed. This dimension, this reality, is the Cross
of Christ. On his Cross the Son of God accomplished the redemption of the
world. It is through this mystery that every cross placed on someone's
shoulders acquires a dignity that is humanly inconceivable and becomes a sign
of salvation for the person who carries it and also for others. 'In my flesh I
complete what is lacking in Christ's afflictions' (Col 1:24), wrote Saint Paul.

Therefore, uniting myself with all of you who are suffering throughout
the land of Poland, in your homes, in the hospitals, the clinics, the
dispensaries, the sanatoria — wherever you may be — I beg you to make use of
the cross that has become part of each one of you for salvation. I pray for you
to have light and spiritual strength in your suffering, that you may not lose
courage but may discover for yourselves the meaning of suffering and may be
able to relieve others by prayer and sacrifice. And do not forget me and the
whole of the Church and the cause of the Gospel and peace that I am serving
by Christ's will. You who are weak and humanly incapable, be a source of
strength for your brother and father who is at your side in prayer and heart.

'Behold, I am the handmaid of the Lord; let it be to me according to your
word' (Lk 1:38).

May these words that Mary is pronouncing by the lips of so many human beings be a light on your path for all of you.

May God reward you, dear brothers and sisters. And God reward all those who are looking after you. Through every manifestation of this care the Word becomes flesh (cf. Jn 1:14). For Christ said: 'As you did it to one of the least of these my brethren, you did it to me' (Mt 25:40).

. . . those warm hearts which glow with evangelical love of one's neighbour

Tuesday 5 June

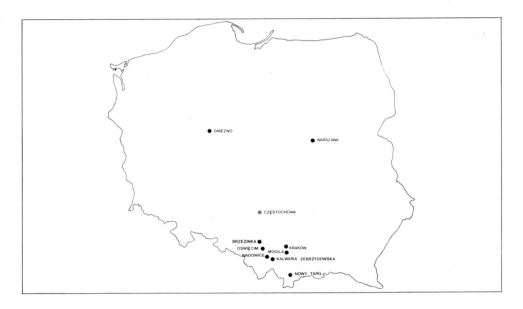

ADDRESS TO POLISH NUNS AT JASNA GÓRA

The Pope arrived at 7.30 a.m. for a reunion with groups of nuns from all parts of Poland on the morning of 5 June, the fourth day of John Paul II's pilgrimage. He spoke to them in the square behind the monastery about the religious vocation 'one of the most noble among those of which the Gospel has spoken and still speaks to us'. He said:

1.   Dear Sisters,

I rejoice with all my heart at this meeting, disposed for us by Divine Providence, today at the feet of Our Lady of Jasna Góra. You have come in such great numbers from all over Poland to participate in the pilgrimage of your fellow-countryman whom Christ in his inscrutable mercy has called, as he once called Simon of Bethsaida, and has commanded him to leave his native land to take upon himself the succession of the Bishops of Rome. Since he has now been given the grace to return again to these parts, he wishes to speak to you with the same words that he used in speaking to you more than once as successor of Saint Stanislaus at Cracow. Those words now take on a different dimension, a universal dimension.

The theme of 'religious vocation' is one of the most beautiful of which the

Gospel has spoken and continues to speak to us. The theme was given a particular incarnation in Mary, who said of herself: 'Behold, I am the handmaid of the Lord; let it be to me according to your word' (Lk 1:38). I think that these words have been echoed in the depths of the religious vocation and profession of each one of you.

2.   While this opportunity to speak to you is being presented to me today, the splendid chapters of the Church's teaching in the last Council come to my mind, as do the very numerous documents of the last Popes.

I would like however, on the basis of all this wealth of teaching by the Church, to refer to some modest statements made by myself. I do so because these statements were echoes of my very numerous past meetings with religious in Poland. These meetings, as a 'resource' of my personal experience, went with me to Rome. It will therefore be perhaps easier for you to find yourselves in those words, for, in spite of having been addressed in other surroundings, they speak in a way of you – of the Polish Sisters and of the Polish religious families.

3.   Soon after my new ministry began I had the good fortune to meet almost twenty thousand sisters from the whole of Rome. Here is a part of the talk that I gave them on that occasion:

Your 'vocation is a special treasure of the Church, which can never cease to pray that the Spirit of Jesus Christ will being forth religious vocations in souls. They are, in fact, both for the community of the People of God, and for the world, a living sign of the future life: a sign which, at the same time, is rooted (also by means of your religious habit) in the everyday life of the Church and of society, and permeates its most delicate tissues. . . .

'(Your presence) must be a visible sign of the Gospel for all. It must also be the source of a particular apostolate. This apostolate is so varied and rich that it is even difficult for me to list here all its forms, its fields, its orientations. It is united with the specific charism of every Congregation, with its apostolic spirit, which the Church and the Holy See approve with joy, seeing in it the expression of the vitality of the Mystical Body of Christ! This apostolate is usually discreet, hidden, near to the human being, and so is more suited to a woman's soul, sensitive to her neighbour, and hence called to the task of a sister and mother.

'It is precisely this vocation which is at the very "heart" of your religious being. As Bishop of Rome I beg you: be spiritually mothers and sisters for all the people of this Church which Jesus, in his ineffable mercy and grace, has wished to entrust to me' (*L'Osservatore Romano*, 12 November 1978, page 16).

4.   On 24 November last I had the occasion to meet the large group of Superiors General gathered in Rome under the leadership of the Cardinal Prefect of the Sacred Congregation for Religious and Secular Institutes. I would like to repeat some phrases from the address I gave on that occasion.

'The religious vocation . . . belongs to that spiritual fullness which the Spirit himself – the Spirit of Christ – brings forth and moulds in the People of God. Without religious orders, without 'consecrated' life, by means of the

vows of chastity, poverty and obedience, the Church would not be fully herself . . . Your houses must be above all centres of prayer, meditation and dialogue – personal and of the whole community – with Him who is and must remain the first and principal interlocutor in the industrious succession of your days. If you are able to nourish this 'climate' of intense and loving community with God, it will be possible for you to carry forward, without traumatic tensions or dangerous confusion, that renewal of life and discipline, to which the Second Vatican Ecumenical Council committed you' (*L'Osservatore Romano*, 25 November 1978, pages 1–2).

5.   Finally, Mexico. The meeting I had in that country's capital remains indelibly inscribed in my memory and my heart. It could not be otherwise, since sisters always create in these meetings a particularly cordial atmosphere and receive with joy the words spoken to them. Here then are some thoughts from the meeting in Mexico:

'Your vocation is one that deserves that highest esteem on the part of the Pope and of the Church, today no less than yesterday. For this reason I wish to express my joyful confidence in you and to encourage you not to lose heart on the way that you have undertaken and which is worth continuing on with fresh spirit and enthusiasm . . . What a lot you can do today for the Church and for humanity! They are waiting for your generous gift, the giving of your free hearts, so that your hearts may broaden their unsuspected potentialities for love in a world that is losing the capacity for altruism, for self-sacrificing and disinterested love. Remember, in fact, that you are mystical brides of Christ and of Christ crucified' (*AAS* 1979, p. 177).

Now let my thoughts and yours turn once again in this place to Our Lady of Jasna Góra, who is the source of living inspiration for each one of you. Let each one of you, as she hears the words spoken at Nazareth, repeat with Mary: 'Behold, I am the handmaid of the Lord; let it be to me according to your word' (Lk 1:38). These words contain in a way the prototype of every religious profession, the profession by which each one of you embraces with her whole being the mystery of the grace transmitted to her in her religious vocation. Each one of you, like Mary, chooses Jesus, the Divine Spouse. By fulfilling her vows of poverty, chastity and obedience, she wishes to live for him, for love of him. Through these vows each one of you wishes to give witness to the eternal life that Christ has brought us in his Cross and Resurrection.

Dear Sisters, this living sign that each one of you constitutes in the midst of humanity is beyond price. Embracing with faith, hope and charity your Divine Spouse, you embrace him in the many people you serve: in the sick, the old, the crippled, the handicapped, people of whom nobody but you is capable of taking care, because this demands a truly heroic sacrifice. Where else do you find Christ? In the children, in young people receiving catechetical instruction, in pastoral service with the priests. You will find him in the simplest service as well as in the tasks that at times demand deep preparation and culture. You will find him everywhere, like the bride of the

Song of Solomon: 'I found him whom my soul loves' (Song 3:4).

May Poland ever rejoice in your evangelical witness. Let there be no want of warm hearts that bring evangelical love to their neighbour. As for you, rejoice always with the joy of your vocation, even when you will have to endure inward or outward suffering or darkness.

Pope John Paul II wishes to pray with you for all this during this Holy Sacrifice.

SPEECH TO THE PLENARY CONFERENCE
OF THE POLISH HIERARCHY

One of the most important
appointments of John Paul II was his
attendance at the 169th Plenary
Assembly of the Polish Episcopal
Conference which took place in the
Library in the Monastery of the Fathers
of the Company of St Paul in Jasna
Góra. The Pope addressed the Polish
bishops as follows:

1.   First of all, I wish to express my joy and deep emotion at our meeting
today. The Polish Bishops' Conference is the community and the setting from
which Christ, by his inscrutable plan, called me on 16 October 1978 to the
See of Saint Peter in Rome, manifesting his will through the votes of the
Sacred College, gathered in Conclave in the Sistine Chapel. As today I have
the good fortune to be taking part again in the plenary assembly of the Polish
Bishops' Conference at Jasna Góra, I cannot fail to express especially my
feelings of gratitude and fraternal solidarity, which go back to the very
beginning of my nomination as a bishop in 1958. I remember that the first
Conference that I took part in as bishop-elect also took place at Jasna Góra, at
the beginning of September.

During the twenty years of my membership and participation in the work
of the Polish Bishops' Conference, I have learned a great deal, both from the
individual members of this episcopal community, beginning with the eminent
Primate of Poland, and also from the community as such. In fact, the quality
that particularly characterizes the Polish Bishops' Conference is that unity
which is the source of spiritual strength. The Polish Episcopate, precisely
through this unity, in a special way serves the Church in Poland and also the
universal Church. Society is well aware of this, and has a justified and
deserved confidence in the Polish Episcopate. This confidence is shown to the
whole of the Episcopate, to all the Archbishops and Bishops in their dioceses,
and especially to the Primate of Poland, of whom I wish to say here what I
have already expressed several times, namely that he is a providential man for
the Church and for the motherland. This is the opinion not only of Poles but
also of people belonging to the other nations of Europe and the world, who
together with us thank the Lord for having given such power to man (cf. Jn
1:12).

During the twenty years of my episcopal ministry, in the course of which
I have been able to serve the Church in Cracow — first at the side of
Archbishop Eugeniusz Baziak of blessed memory (Metropolitan of the
orphaned Archdiocese of Lwow), then as the successor of the Metropolitan of
Cracow, Cardinal Adam Stefan Sapieha in the See of Saint Stanislaus — there
have accumulated in my heart great debts of gratitude, debts which I seek to
repay, as best I can, with remembrance of and prayer for the Polish Cardinals,
Archbishops and Bishops, living and dead. Those who have died do not fade
from my memory, especially those with whom it has been granted to me to
be closest to, by working with them, in the range of the influence of their
personalities, as in the case of the Archbishops of Cracow I have mentioned,

74

the late Cardinal Boleslaw Kominek, Metropolitan of Wroclaw, Archbishop Anthony Baraniak, Metropolitan of Poznań, and so many magnificent and unforgettable Bishops, both Ordinaries and Auxiliaries, men full of human originality and Christian authenticity, whom the Lord has called to himself during these twenty years. I cannot fail to recall the late Cardinal Boleslaw Filipiak, who for many years of his life served the Holy See, and whom I met many times in Rome.

Taking part in the work of the Polish Episcopate has enabled me to study at close quarters the problems of the modern Church in their universal dimensions. This has occurred thanks in particular to the Council, which I had the good fortune to take part in from the first day to the last. In entering into all this vast combination of problems, which Vatican II pinpointed in all its documents, I have been able to realize what a special and responsible place Poland, and especially the Church in Poland, has on the great map of the modern world, that world to which we are sent as the Apostles were sent at the moment of Christ's Ascension, with the words: 'Go therefore and make disciples of all nations' (Mt 28:19). This realization became even deeper during the years following the Council, thanks especially to work in the Synod of Bishops, in the Congregations of the Apostolic See, and thanks also to my meetings with representatives of the various Episcopates, both from Europe and from the other continents. One of the opportunities consisted in the visits to *emigré* Poles which I made several times in the name of the Polish Episcopate.

Today I remember all this with gratitude. My membership of the Polish Episcopal Conference and my many-sided participation in its work has been confirmed by Providence as the most appropriate means of preparation for that ministry which since 16 October I have had to exercise *vis-à-vis* the whole universal Church. I wish to say this at the beginning of my address, which is being given to this unusual plenary meeting of the Polish Episcopal Conference taking place here today.

2. In the Church in my motherland, the year 1979 is the year of Saint Stanislaus. Nine hundred years have passed since his death at the hands of King Boleslaw the Bold at Skalka. The death of the Bishop who proclaimed to everyone — not excluding the King — the truth of the faith and of Christian morality had a significance of special witness to the Gospel and to Christ himself. Stanislaus of Szczepanow suffered death in such manner that, in the Church's tradition, he was included among the martyrs. At the beginning of our history, in the second century of Christianity in Poland, that martyr Bishop, blood of the blood and bone of the bone of the nation, was linked with another martyr Bishop, one who belonged to the first missionary generation and the time of the Baptism — Saint Wojciech (Adalbert), who was of Czech origin. I mention him because, in the memory of the People of God on Polish soil, these two figures are linked together and surrounded by a special veneration and devotion.

Stanislaus of Szczepanow was Bishop of Cracow and a member of the Polish Episcopate at that time, and therefore the present Polish Episcopate has particular reasons for surrounding his figure with special veneration, and especially the anniversary of his martyrdom. This has been taking place in the Archdiocese of Cracow since 1972, while in the Diocese of Tarnow, where Szczepanow, the Saint's birthplace, is situated, they are celebrating the 'Year of Saint Stanislaus'. As Bishop and pastor of the See of Cracow, Saint Stanislaus was one of the pillars of that hierarchical order which was established in the lands of the Piasts from the year 1000. We have special reasons for continually thanking God for the solid foundations of that order, instituted during the Congress of Gniezno upon the foundation of the apostolic mission of Saint Wojciech and his martyrdom. It was precisely to that martyred body, which Boleslaw the Bold translated with veneration to Gniezno, that the legates of Pope Silvester II and the Emperor Otto III came. The Poland of the Piasts, which from as early as 968 *cepit habere episcopum* at Poznań — relatively early, because it was scarcely 34 years after the baptism of Mieszko — gained its own ecclesiastical organization: the metropolitan see at Gniezno with episcopal sees at Cracow, Wroclaw and Kolobrzeg.

These facts are known by everyone. But it is impossible to fail to recall them and to refer to them on this extraordinary occasion that we are experiencing together.

The hierarchical order is a constitutive element of Christ's Church, as the Dogmatic Constitution on the Church, *Lumen Gentium*, authoritatively reminded us. The Church, which as the People of God has been built up upon the mystery of the Incarnation and Redemption, and which is continually born from the descent of the Holy Spirit, is the visible reality of a clearly defined hierarchical order. This order determines the Church as a well defined community and society, which through its own hierarchical order forms part of the history of humanity, in the history of the individual peoples and nations. Therefore we rightly venerate Saint Wojciech as the patron of the hierarchical order in our motherland. We rightly recall and appreciate the great leaders of the Assembly of Gniezno. Through the formal hierarchical structure that she gained in Poland at that time, the Church firmly became part of the nation's history. The year 1000 is a date that with good reason we link to the date of the Baptism that took place in 966.

Knowledge of the history of Poland will tell us still more: not only has the hierarchical order of the Church decisively inserted into the history of the nation in 1000, but also the history of the nation was in a providential manner rooted in the structure of the Church in Poland, a structure that we owe to the Assembly of Gniezno. This affirmation finds its confirmation in the various periods of the history of Poland, and particularly in the most difficult periods. When national and State structures were lacking, society, for the most part Catholic, found support in the hierarchical order of the Church. And this helped society to overcome the times of the partition of the country and the times of occupation; it helped society to maintain, and even to deepen its understanding of, the awareness of its own identity. Perhaps certain people from other countries may consider this situation 'untypical', but for the Poles it has an unmistakable eloquence. It is simply a part of the truth of the history of our own motherland.

The Episcopate of modern Poland is in a special way the heir and representative of this truth. There is a deep reason for the fact that for a thousand years of history the heritage of the holy martyr bishops Wojciech and Stanislaus has permeated the thoughts and the hearts of the Poles.

3.   When in the year 1000 there arose in Poland the fundamental structure of the hierarchical order of the Church, it arose, right from the beginning, in the unity of the hierarchy with the order of the universal Church — that is to say with the Apostolic See. In this relationship the structure of the Church has lasted uninterruptedly in our motherland up till today. Thanks to this, Poland is Catholic and 'ever faithful'. The unity of the hierarchical structure, the bond between the Polish Episcopate and the See of Peter, constitutes the basis of this unity in its universal dimension. The Church in Poland, throughout the centuries, has been firmly and unshakably rooted in that universality which is one of the marks of Christ's Church. The Constitution *Lumen Gentium* exhaustively studied this fact under various aspects, at the same time showing how the universal dimension of the Church is linked to the mission and ministry of Peter.

We are well aware that this fact that the Church in Poland is rooted in its catholicity — from the moment of the Baptism and of the Assembly of Gniezno and throughout history — has a particular meaning for the spiritual life of the nation. And it also has a meaning for the nation's culture, which is marked not only by the tradition of visible links with Rome, but also possesses the characteristic of universality proper to Catholicism and the characteristic of openness to everything which in the universal exchange of good things becomes the portion of each of those who take part in it. This affirmation could be confirmed by innumerable instances taken from our history. One of these instances could also be the fact that we are together today, namely that the Polish Episcopate is meeting a Polish Pope.

It is generally stated that the Polish people's sharing in the Church's spiritual heritage, which results from its universal unity, has become an element of unity and security of the nation's identity and unity in the particularly difficult periods. Those periods were also particularly marked by the spreading of the Christian spirit. This is confirmed by the nineteenth century, and for us it is confirmed by the recent decades of the present century. After the period of occupation, which as everyone knows was a terrible and mortal threat for Poland's survival, there began a period of great transformations which found outward expression, for example, in the completely new definition of the boundaries of the State.

In this context, the bond between the life of the nation and the activity of the Church, a bond experienced for centuries, has been once more activated before our eyes. The normalization of ecclesiastical relationships in the sphere of the new boundaries of the Polish State, and in particular in the territories of the West and North, has clearly confirmed the meaning of the year 1000 or the times of Saints Wojciech and Stanislaus. The hierarchical order of the State has become not only the centre of her pastoral mission, but also a clear support for the whole life of society, for the nation conscious of its right to exist, which, as a nation that is in the vast majority Catholic, seeks this support also in the hierarchical structures of the Church. Such is the eloquence of the events that began in the pontificate of Pope Pius XII in

1945, shortly after the end of the War and the Occupation, with the memorable mission of Cardinal Augustyn Hlond, Primate of Poland, and concluded with the final decisions of Pope Paul VI in June 1972, when in the Archdiocese of Cracow there began the seven-year jubilee of the pastoral service of Saint Stanislaus. It is significant that it was precisely during the Plenary Conference in Cracow, on 28 June, that these important decisions of Paul VI were made public.

The Church's hierarchical order finds its keystone in the mission and ministry of Peter. The Apostolic See draws from this mission and ministry the character that is proper to it. This character is not one of secular and political structure, even though, for reasons that are still valid, there is still linked to the See of Rome a remnant of the old Papal States. However, as in the case of that State, which in its historical aspect ceased to exist in 1870, so likewise the one which actually remains of it and which is only symbolical, is a guarantee of the sovereignty of the Apostolic See in regard to the world and constitutes a basis to support what is essential for the Apostolic See. This stems solely and exclusively from the nature of the Church, from her apostolic mission, from the evangelical service to truth and love, from the pastoral mission which above all the hierarchical order of the Church serves. The chapters devoted to this hierarchical order and its motivation are found in the Constitution *Lumen Gentium*, after the chapters dealing with the mystery of the Church and the universal mission of the People of God.

It is only if we keep before our eyes this proper and correct image of the Church, and, in its organic whole, the proper image of the Apostolic See, that we can lay down exactly the meaning of the question that for many years has been of great relevance in Poland — the question of the normalization of relations between the Church and the State. It is necessary to speak here about this relevance which has new aspects, becuase the already-mentioned question has behind it, for understandable reasons, a long and complex history which cannot be ignored. The Polish Episcopate, in close collaboration with the Apostolic See, especially during the pontificate of John XXIII and Paul VI, did a great deal for the cause of this normalization. In the first place, it laid down a series of concrete elements on which to base it. Of fundamental assistance in this pioneering work was the teaching contained in the documents of the Second Vatican Council; and especially the possibility of using the 'Declaration on Religious Freedom', a document that directly tallies with the principles promulgated in fundamental State and international documents, including the Constitution of the Polish People's Republic. It is clear that the concrete application of these principles can only respond to the idea of 'religious freedom' when it takes into consideration the real needs of the Church linked with her many-sided activity.

I spoke about this subject, and also of the Church's readiness to collaborate with all countries and with all people of good will, on 12 January last to the Diplomatic Corps accredited to the Holy See. Here is a relevant passage:

'Maintaining contacts — among others by means of diplomatic representations — with so many and such different States, the Apostolic See wishes above all to express its deep esteem for each nation and each people, for its tradition, its culture, its progress in every field, as I said already in the letters addressed to Heads of State on the occasion of my election to the See of Peter. The State, as the expression of the sovereign self determination of peoples and nations, is a normal realization of social order. Its moral authority consists in that. The son of a people with a millenary culture which was deprived for a considerable time of its independence as a State, I know, from experience, the deep significance of this principle.

'The Apostolic See welcomes joyfully all diplomatic representatives, not only as spokesmen of their own governments, regimes and political structures, but also and above all as representatives of peoples and nations which, through these political structures, manifest their sovereignty, their political independence, and the possibility of deciding their destiny autonomously. And it does so without any prejudice as regards the numerical importance of the population: here, it is not the numerical factor that is decisive.

'The Apostolic See rejoices at the presence of so many representatives; it would likewise be happy to see many others, especially of nations and peoples which at times had a centuries-old tradition in this connection. I am thinking here particularly of the nations that can be considered Catholic; but also of others. For, at present, just as ecumenism between the Catholic Church and other Christian Churches is developing, just as there is a tendency to establish contacts with all men by appealing to good will, so this circle is widening . . . The Apostolic See, in conformity with the mission of the Church, wishes to be at the centre of this brotherly *rapprochement*. It wishes to serve the cause of peace, not through political activity, but by serving the values and principles which condition peace and *rapprochement*, and which are at the basis of the international common good . . .

'We see clearly that humanity is divided in a great many ways. It is a question also, and perhaps above all, of ideological divisions bound up with the different State systems. The search for solutions that will permit human societies to carry out their own tasks and to live in justice, is perhaps the main sign of our time . . . Advantage must be taken of mutual experiences . . . 'The Apostolic See, which has already given proof of this, is always ready to manifest its openness with regard to all countries or regimes, seeking the essential good which is man's real good. A good number of exigencies connected with this good have been expressed in the "Declaration of Human Rights" and in the international Pacts which permit its concrete application' (*AAS* 70, 1978, pp. 170–179).

The Polish Episcopate has its own experiences in this important field. Basing itself on the teaching of Vatican II, it has worked out a series of documents of theory, which are known to the Apostolic See, and at the same time it has worked out a series of pastoral attitudes that confirm readiness for dialogue. They clearly show that authentic dialogue must respect the convictions of believers, ensure all the rights of citizens and also the normal conditions for the activity of the Church as a religious community to which the vast majority of Poles belong. We are aware that this dialogue cannot be easy, because it takes place between two concepts of the world which are diametrically opposed; but it must be possible and effective if the good of individuals and the nation demands it. The Polish Episcopate must not cease

to undertake with solicitude initiatives which are important for the present-day Church. In addition, in the future there must be clarity in the principles of procedure which in the present situation have been worked out within the ecclesial community, regarding both the attitude of clergy and lay people and the status of individual institutions. Clarity of principles, as also their practical putting into effect, is a source of moral strength and also serves the process of a true normalization.

In favour of the normalization of Church-State relations in our time, the cause of fundamental human rights, including the right to religious liberty, has an undoubted significance, which under a certain aspect is fundamental and central. The normalization of Church-State relations constitutes a practical proof of respect for this right and for all its consequences in the life of the political community. Thought of in this way, normalization is also a practical manifestation of the fact that the State understands its mission to society according to the principle of subsidiarity (*principium subsidiarietatis*), namely that it wishes to express the full sovereignty of the nation. In relation to the Polish Nation, with regard to its special millenary and the present connection with the Catholic Church, this last aspect takes on a particular significance.

4.   Throughout this consideration, especially in its last part, we have penetrated deeply into the sphere of the ethical reasons that make up the fundamental dimension of human life, also in the field of that activity that is called political. In conformity with the tradition of European thought, which goes back to the works of the greatest philosophers of antiquity and which found its full confirmation and deeper development in the Gospel and in Christianity, political activity also — indeed especially — finds its proper meaning in solicitude for people's good, which is a good of an ethnical nature. From here that whole so-called social teaching of the Church derives its deepest premises, a teaching that, especially in our time, beginning from the end of the nineteenth century, has been enormously enriched by all the problems of the present day. This does not mean that the Church's social teaching appeared only at the turn of the century; in fact it existed from the beginning, as a consequence of the Gospel and of the vision of man that the Gospel brought into relationships with other people, and especially in community and social life.

Saint Stanislaus is called the patron of the moral order in Poland. Perhaps it is precisely in him that we see most clearly how deeply the moral order penetrates — the moral order which is so fundamental for man, the *humanum* — in the structures and levels of the life of the nation as a State, in the structures and levels of political life. We can never meditate too deeply about the way in which that holy Bishop of Cracow, who suffered death at the hand of an eminent representative of the Piast dynasty, was later well received, especially in the thirteenth century, by the successors of the same dynasty, and later, after his canonization in 1253, venerated as Patron of the unity of the motherland, which by reason of dynastic divisions found itself split up. Certainly, this unusual tradition of the cult of Saint Stanislaus throws a special light on the events of 1079, during which the Bishop of Cracow suffered death, while King Boleslaw the Bold lost his crown and was forced to leave Poland. And even though Gall the Anonymous, writing his chronicle some decades later, used with regard to Bishop Stanislaus the expression traditor, this or similar expressions are found at that time applied for various other Bishops (as for example Saint Thomas Becket in England) and even to Popes (for example Saint Gregory VII), who earned the halo of sainthood. Obviously, the episcopal ministry has sometimes exposed Bishops to the peril of losing their lives and thus of paying the price of proclaiming the truth and the divine law.

The fact that Saint Stanislaus, whom history calls 'the Patron of the Poles', has been recognized by the Polish Episcopate especially as Patron of the moral order finds its motivation in the eloquent ethical value of his life and death, and also in the whole tradition that has expressed itself throughout the generations of the Poland of the Piasts, of the Jagellonians and of the elected kings, down to our own times. The patronage of the moral order that we attribute to Saint Stanislaus is principally linked with the universal recognition of authority, of the moral law, that is to say of the law of God. This law places an obligation upon everyone, both subjects and rulers. It constitutes the moral norm, and is an essential criterion of man's value. Only when we begin from this law, namely the moral law, can the dignity of the human person be respected and universally recognized. Therefore, morality and law are the fundamental conditions for social order. Upon the law are built States and nations, and without it they perish.

The Polish Episcopate, with a deep sense of responsibility for the nation's destiny, always points out, in its pastoral programmes, the sum of threats of a moral nature which the man of our time, the man of modern civilization, fights against. These threats relate both to personal life and to life in society, and they weigh especially heavily upon the family and upon the education of the young. Married people, the family nuclei, must be defended from sin, from grave sin against nascent life. In fact it is well known that the circumstances of that sin weigh upon the morality of society, and its consequences menace the future of the nation. And then one must defend people from the sins of immorality and alcoholic abuse, because these sins bear within them the lowering of human dignity, and have incalculable consequences in the life of society. Watchfulness is always needed, human consciences must always be kept alert, warnings must always be given in the face of violation of moral principles, people must be urged to carry out the commandment of charity, for inner insensitivity easily takes root in human hearts.

This is the eternal problem that has not only not lost its relevance in our times but has become even more clear and obvious. The Church needs a hierarchical order if she is to serve people and society effectively in the field of the moral order. Saint Stanislaus is the expression, symbol and patron of this order. Given that the moral order is at the basis of all human culture, the national tradition rightly sees Saint Stanislaus's place at the basis of Polish culture. The Polish Episcopate must add to its present mission and ministry a particular solicitude for the whole Polish cultural heritage, of which we know to what degree it is permeated by the light of Christianity. It is also well known that it is precisely culture that is the first and fundamental proof of the nation's identity. The mission of the Polish Episcopate, inasmuch as it is the continuation of the mission of Saint Stanislaus, is in a certain manner marked by his historical charism — and therefore remains in this field clear and irreplaceable.

5.   It is hard to think of our great Jubilee of the nine hundredth anniversary of the death of Saint Stanislaus and to prescind from the European context. Just as it is hard to think of and live the Millennium of the Baptism of Poland without referring to that context. Today, that context has widened beyond Europe, especially because the sons and daughters of so many European nations — including the Poles — have populated and formed the life of society in other continents. Yet there the European context is undoubtedly at the very basis. The already mentioned analogies of the cause of Saint Stanislaus with those of other nations and States, of the same historical period, clearly show how the Poland of the eleventh century formed part of Europe and shared in its problems, both in the life of the Church and in the life of the political communities of that time. And so it is that we are rightly living the Jubilee of Saint Stanislaus, a Jubilee that has above all a Polish and native dimension, in the European context. We cannot do otherwise. Therefore, the presence of the Representatives of the many European Episcopal Conferences who have come here for the occasion is highly valued and eloquent.

It providentially happened that on 18 May of this year I took part in the celebration of the 35th anniversary of the battle of Monte Cassino and the victory won there, a victory to which my fellow-countrymen contributed in great measure. On the same Monte Cassino we paid tribute to Saint Benedict, with reference to the coming 1500th anniversary of his birth — that Saint Benedict who was proclaimed Patron of Europe by Paul VI.

If I may allow myself to make this reference on today's occasion, I do so in relation to the European context of Saint Stanislaus and also of his Jubilee that we are celebrating. Europe, which during its history has been several times divided, Europe, which towards the end of the first half of the present century was tragically divided by the horrible World War, Europe, which despite its present and long-wasting divisions of regimes, ideologies and economical and political systems, cannot cease to seek its fundamental unity, must turn to Christianity. Despite the different traditions that exist in the territory of Europe between its Eastern part and its Western part, there lives in each of them the same Christianity, which takes its origins from the same Christ, which accepts the same Word of God, which is linked with the same Twelve Apostles. Precisely this lies at the roots of the history of Europe. This forms its spiritual genealogy.

This is confirmed by the eloquence of the present Jubilee of Saint Stanislaus, Patron of Poland, in which the first Polish Pope, the first Slav Pope in the history of the Church and of Europe, has the good fortune to be taking part. Christianity must commit itself anew to the formation of the spiritual unity of Europe. Economic and political reasons alone cannot do it.

The Polish Episcopate, all the Episcopates and Churches in Europe, have here a great task to perform. In the face of these many-sided tasks, the Apostolic See is aware of its own tasks in conformity with the character and ministry of Peter. When Christ said: 'Strengthen your brethren' (Lk 22:32) he meant by this: 'Serve their unity'.

ADDRESS TO THE POLISH HIERARCHY'S COUNCIL FOR SCIENCE

At the conclusion of the 169th Plenary Conference of the Polish Episcopacy, John Paul II met the Bishops' Council for Science and addressed them as follows:

It is with great joy that I meet the venerable Council for Science of the Polish Episcopate, of which, until a short time ago, by reason of the will of the Conference of the same Episcopate, I was the chairman. Today I cordially greet my successor, Bishop Marian Rechowicz, all the dear priests and professors.

I wish to tell you that I now give the same importance as before to the Council for Science of the Episcopate. Perhaps, indeed, after the promulgation of the new Apostolic Constitution *Sapientia Christiana* on university studies, I see more clearly the relevance of our Council for Science and appreciate with greater understanding its function and responsibility.

The Church — particularly in our time — must face this responsibility. It must first of all decide knowledgeably about the problems of its own science at the academic level. It must likewise, with great awareness, participate in the important processes of contemporary science that are linked to the activities of the universities and the various institutes, especially its own universities and its own Catholic institutes.

The Council for Science of the Episcopate, which comprises the representatives of all the Catholic Athenaea of an academic character in Poland, must precisely in this field be useful to the Episcopate and to the Church in our motherland. I do not exaggerate if I say that upon it falls in great part the responsibility for Christian Polish culture today and tomorrow.

And taking account therefore of all this, I recommend the future activities of all of you, Bishops and Professors, to Mary, Seat of Divine Wisdom, and with all my heart I bless you.

THE RECITAL OF THE *ANGELUS* WITH THE POPE

A vast crowd was present, at midday on
5 June, at the Sanctuary of the
Madonna of Częstochowa to recite the
Angelus Domini with the Pope. Before
doing so, he talked to them about this
prayer.

1.   In Rome there is a beautiful custom that on every Sunday and holy day
the Pope recites the Angelus with the faithful gathered in Saint Peter's
Square. I inherited this custom from my venerable predecessors and I continue
it with great joy. The prayer is preceded by a short meditation and a mention
of certain events which need to be particularly recommended to God in
prayer, and we conclude with a blessing.

My fellow-countrymen in Poland are acquainted with this Roman
practice. In fact, from the time I was called to the Chair of Peter, they began
spontaneously to join with me in reciting the Angelus every day at the usual
hours of the morning, at midday and in the evening. The recitation of this
prayer has become a universal practice, testified to by numerous letters and
mentions in the press. Through the Angelus we are spiritually linked
together, we remember each other and we share the mystery of salvation and
our hearts also.

Today, while reciting the Angelus at Jasna Góra, I wish to thank all my
fellow-countrymen in all of Poland for their worthy initiative. I have always
been deeply moved by your constant remembrance of me and now I wish to
express this feeling publicly.

2.   At the same time, I wish, together with you my dear brothers and
sisters, to ask our Most Holy Mother that the praying of the Angelus may be
a constant reminder to one and all of how great is the dignity of man. This,
in fact, is the fruit and the goal of this prayer. Remembering that 'the Word
became flesh', that is, that the Son of God became man, we must become
conscious of how great each man has become through this mystery, through
the Incarnation of the Son of God! Christ, in fact, was conceived in the womb
of Mary and became man to reveal the eternal love of the Creator and Father
and to make known the dignity of each one of us.

If we regularly pray the Angelus, this prayer must influence all our
conduct. We cannot recite it only with our lips; we cannot repeat the
Angelus and at the same time act in a way which clashes with our human and
Christian dignity.

I shall not now speak in detail of everything in the attitude of Poles that
is opposed to the dignity of 'God's image and likeness', the dignity that was
confirmed by the mystery of the Incarnation. We know very well the voices

that at times become real plagues threatening the spiritual and biological life of the nation. Think of it, dear brothers and sisters. I heartily beg you to do so.

Continue, then, to recite the Angelus with the Pope. May it bear fruit in every aspect of the life of the Polish people, not only on holy days but every day of their lives.

SERMON TO PILGRIMS FROM LOWER SILESIA AND OPOLE

About a million of the faithful from Lower Silesia and Opole were gathered at the monastery of Jasna Góra during the afternoon to take part with the Pope in a celebration of the Mass which was sung by the Archbishop of Wrocław, Henryk Gulbinowich. John Paul II preached the following sermon:

1.   From Jasna Góra I wish to present a special votive offering to the shrine of Saint Hedwig in Trzebnica near Wrocklaw. I have a special reason for doing so. In its inscrutable designs Divine Providence chose 16 October 1978 as a turning point in my life. On 16 October the Church in Poland celebrates Saint Hedwig, and for that reason I feel specially bound to make this votive offering today to the Church in Poland for the Saint who, as well as being the patroness of reconciliation between the neighbouring countries, is also the saint honoured on the day of the election of the first Pole to the Chair of Peter. I place this votive offering directly in the hands of all the pilgrims who have come today in such large numbers to Jasna Góra from all over Lower Silesia. I ask you, after your return to your province, to take this votive offering from the Pope to the shrine of Trzebnica, which became the new homeland that she chose for herself. Let it thus complete the long history of human events and works of Divine Providence connected with Trzebnica and all your region.

2.   Saint Hedwig, the wife of Henry the Bearded, of the Piast dynasty, came from the Bavarian family Andechs. She entered our country's history and indirectly the history of the whole of Europe in the thirteenth century as the 'good wife' (Prov 31:10) of which Scripture speaks. Our memories have specially engraved on them the event dominated by the figure of her son, Prince Henry the Pious. He it was who put up a strong resistance to the Tartar invasion that passed in 1241 through Poland from the East, from Asia, and stopping only in Silesia near Legnica. Henry the Pious fell, it is true, on the battlefield, but the Tartars were forced to retire and they never again came so close to the West in their raids. Behind the heroic son was his mother, who gave him courage and recommended to the Crucified Christ the battle of Legnica. Her heart paid with the death of her son for the peace and security of the lands subject to her and also of the neighbouring lands and the whole of Western Europe.

During these occurrences Hedwig was already a widow, and as a widow she consecrated the rest of her life exclusively to God, entering the abbey of Trzebnica, which had been founded by her. Here she ended her holy life in 1243. Her canonization took place in 1267. This date is very close to that of the canonization in 1253 of Saint Stanislaus, the saint venerated by the Church in Poland for centuries as its principal Patron.

This year, on the occasion of the ninth centenary of his martyrdom at

Shalka in Cracow, I, as the first Pope who am a son of the Polish nation, who was formerly Saint Stanislaus's successor on the Chair of Cracow and have now been elected to the Chair of Saint Peter on Saint Hedwig's Day — I wish to send to her shrine of Trzebnica this votive offering from me marking a further stage in the centuries of history in which we all share.

3. To my votive offering I add my specially cordial good wishes for all taking part in this Sacred Eucharist that I am celebrating today at Jasna Góra. The Saints whom we are commemorating here today before Our Lady of Jasna Góra offer us across the centuries a witness of unity between fellow-countrymen and of reconciliation between nations. I want to express my good wishes for this unity and reconciliation. For this I pray ardently.

Unity strikes root in the life of the nation, as in the difficult historical period for Poland it struck root through Saint Stanislaus, when human life at the various levels responds to the demands of justice and love. The family constitutes the first of these levels. And I wish to pray today with all of you, dear fellow-countrymen, for the unity of all the families of Poland. This unity has its origin in the sacrament of Marriage, in the solmen promises with which a man and a woman become united with each other for the whole of life, repeating the sacramental 'till death do us part'. Thus unity comes from love and mutual trust and bears fruit in the love and trust of the children towards their parents. What a misfortune it would be if love and trust between husband and wife or between parents and children should weaken or crumble. Aware as we are of the evil brought by the falling apart of the family, let us today pray that nothing may happen which can destroy its unity, so that the family may continue to be truly 'the seat of justice and love'.

Similar justice and love are needed by the nation, if it is to be inwardly united, if it is to constitute an unbreakable unity. Although it is impossible to compare the nation — that society composed of many millions of people — with the family — the smallest community, as we know, of human society — nevertheless unity depends on justice, a justice that satisfied the needs and guarantees the rights and duties of each member of the nation, so as not to give rise to disharmony and opposition because of the differences brought by evident privileges for some and discrimination against others. From our country's history we know how difficult this task is; all the same we cannot exempt ourselves from the great effort aimed at building up just unity between the children of the same country. This must be accompanied by love for this country, love for its culture and its history, love for its specific values that determine its place in the great family of nations, love, finally, for our fellow-countrymen, people who speak the same language and have responsibility for the common cause to which we give the name of 'our country'.

As I pray today together with you for the internal unity of the nation of which Saint Stanislaus became Patron, especially in the thirteenth and fourteenth centuries, I wish to recommend to the Mother of God in Jasna Góra reconciliation between the nations, of which reconciliation we see one mediating in the figure of Saint Hedwig. As inward unity within each society or community, whether a nation or a family, depends on respect for the rights of each of its members, so international reconciliation depends on recognition of and respect for the rights of each nation. Chief of these rights are the rights to existence and self-determination, to its own culture and the many forms of developing it. We know from our own country's history what has been the cost to us of the infraction, the violation and the denial of those inalienable rights. Let us therefore pray with greater enthusiasm for lasting reconciliation between the nations of Europe and the world. May this be the fruit of recognition of and real respect for the rights of each nation.

4.   The Church wishes to place herself at the service of unity among people; she desires to place herself at the service of reconciliation between nations. This belongs to her saving mission. Let us continually open our thoughts and hearts to the peace of which the Lord Jesus so often spoke to the Apostles, both before his Passion and after his Resurrection: 'I leave you peace, my peace I give you' (Jn 14:27).

May this Pope who is today speaking here on the height of Jasna Góra effectively serve the cause of unity and reconciliation in the modern world. In this task keep assisting him with your prayers throughout the land of Poland.

THE INVOCATION OF JASNA GÓRA

Every evening at 9 p.m. the Sanctuary
of Jasna Góra is the goal of a
procession of the faithful who visit the
monastery in order to recite the
'Invocation of Jasna Góra', a prayer
which unites them spiritually with Poles
throughout the world. The Holy Father
led the prayer and when he had
finished reciting it with the hundreds of
thousands of believers who were
present, he addressed them as follows:

1.   'Mary, Queen of Poland, I am close to you, I remember you, I watch!'
    Within a short time we shall repeat these words which, from the time of
the Great Novena in preparation for the Millennium of the Baptism, have
become the call of Jasna Góra and of the Church in Poland.
    I shall repeat them today with you as the pilgrim Pope in his native land.
    How greatly these words correspond to the invitation which we hear so
often in the Gospel: 'Be watchful!' By answering this invitation of Christ
himself we desire today as every evening at the hour of the call of Jasna Góra,
to say to Mary: 'Mary, Queen of Poland, I am close to you, I remember you,
I watch'.
    These words, simple yet forceful, express what it means to be a Christian
in Poland at all times, but in a special way during this decisive millenary
period of the history of the Church and of the nation. To be a Christian is to
be watchful, as the soldier is watchful, as a mother is with her child, a doctor
with his patient.
    To be watchful means to protect something of great value.
    On the occasion on the Millennium of the Baptism we have become
aware, to an even greater extent, of the great good which is our faith and of
all that spiritual heritage which has come from it in the course of our history.
To be watchful means to guard all of this. It means to have an acute
awareness of the values which are inherent in the life of every human being,
simply because he is a human being created in the image and likeness of God
and redeemed by the Blood of Christ. To be watchful means to remember all
of this. To remember it for ourselves and often even for others, for our
fellow-citizens, for our neighbour.

2.   We must be watchful, dear brothers and sisters, we must be watchful
and solicitous for the entire well-being of every man, because this is the great
incumbent on all of us. We cannot permit the loss of what is human, Polish
and Christian on this earth.
    'Be sober, be watchful' (1 Pt 5:8), says Saint Peter; and I today, at the
hour of the call of Jasna Góra, repeat his words. Indeed, I find myself here in
order to watch with you in this hour and to show you how deeply I feel every
threat against man, against the family and the nation. A threat that always
has its source in our human weakness, in a fragile will and in a superficial

way of looking at life. And therefore, fellow-countrymen, in this hour of particular sincerity, in this hour of the opening of our hearts before Our Lady of Jasna Góra, I am speaking to you about this, and this is what I am entrusting to you. Do not succumb to weakness!

'Do not be overcome by evil, but overcome evil with good' (Rom 12:21). If you see that your brother is falling, help him; do not leave him exposed to the risk! Sometimes it is difficult to support the other person, especially if 'he is slipping from our hands.' But can this be done? It is God himself, it is Christ himself who entrusts to us each one of our brothers and sisters, each one of our fellow-countrymen, saying '. . . as often as you did it for one of my least brethren, you did it for me' (Mt 25:40). Be careful not to make yourselves responsible for the sins of others! Christ addresses severe words to those who give scandal (cf. Mt 18:6–7). Reflect, therefore, dear brother or sister, in this hour of national sincerity, in the presence of the Mother and her heart full of love, whether you do not give scandal, whether you do not induce someone to evil, whether through a lack of responsibility you do not burden your conscience with vices and with bad habits that others contract because of you . . . the young people . . . perhaps your own children.

'Be sober, be watchful!'

To be watchful and to remember in this way is to stand next to Mary. I am close to you! I cannot be close to you, to Our Lady of Jasna Góra, unless I am watchful and I remember in this way. If I watch and I remember, then I am close to her. And because she has so penetrated into our hearts it is easier for us to be watchful and remember what is our heritage and our duty, standing next to Mary. 'I am near you'.

3.   The call of Jasna Góra has not ceased to be our prayer and our programme! The prayer and programme of all! May it be in particular the prayer and the programme of Polish families!

The family is the first and basic human community. It is a sphere of life, it is a sphere of love. The life of every society, nation and State depends on the family, on whether the family is a true sphere of life and love in their midst. Much has to be done; indeed, everything possible has to be done, to give to the family those means that it needs: means for employment, means for housing, means to support itself, care for life which has been conceived, social respect for fatherhood and motherhood, the joy given by children born into the world, the full right to education and at the same time the various types of help needed for education . . . Here is a vast and rich programme on which depends the future of the individual and of the nation.

How I desire today, my dear fellow-countrymen, how ardently I desire that in this programme there should be fulfilled day after day, year after year, the call of Jasna Góra, the prayer of Polish hearts.

How ardently I desire, I who owe my life, my faith, my language to a Polish family, that the family should never cease to be strong with the strength of God. May it overcome whatever weakens it or tears it assunder; may it overcome whatever does not permit it to be a true sphere of life and love. For this I pray for you now with the words of the call of Jasna Góra.

And I wish to pray also in the future, repeating: 'I am close to you, I remember you, I watch', until this cry before the Mother of God rebounds and becomes a reality where it is needed most.

Where, on fidelity to these words repeated at the end of the first Millennium there will depend to a great extent the new Millennium.

Monstra Te esse Matrem

Wednesday 6 June

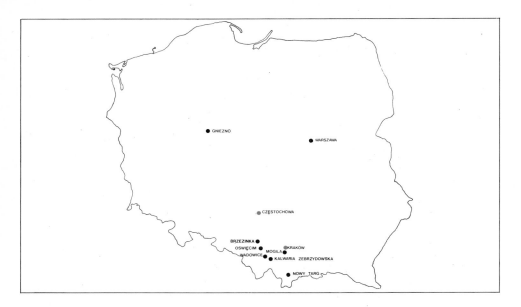

THE ADDRESS TO SEMINARISTS AT JASNA GÓRA

'I entrust every religious vocation to Our Lady of Jasna Góra.' John Paul II spoke these words to a gathering of seminarists, novices and members of the minor orders for whom he said Mass at 8 a.m. in the sanctuary on the morning of Wednesday 6 June. To an audience of several thousand, the Pope spoke as follows:

My dear friends!

1.   The Gospel which we often hear read when we are present here at Jasna Góra is that which recalls the wedding feast at Cana of Galilee. Saint John as an eye witness has described that event in all its particulars — an event which took place at the beginning of the public life of Christ the Lord. This is the first miracle — the first sign of the saving power of Christ — performed in the presence of his Mother and his first disciples, the future Apostles.

You also are gathered here as disciples of Christ the Lord. Each one of you has become his disciple through holy Baptism, which requires a solid preparation of our minds, our wills and our hearts. This is done by means of catechesis, first of all in our families, then in the parish. By catechesis we search ever more deeply into the mystery of Christ and we discover the meaning of our participation in it. Catechesis is not only learning religious concepts; it is an introduction to the life of participation in the mystery of Christ. Thus, knowing Christ — and through him also the Father: 'He who has seen me has seen the Father' (Jn 14:9) — we become, in the Holy Spirit, participants in the new life which Christ has grafted into us from the moment of Baptism and which he has strengthened with Confirmation.

2.   This new life which Christ has given us becomes our spiritual life, our interior life. We therefore discover within ourselves the interior person with its qualities, talents, worthy desires and ideals; but we also discover our weaknesses, our vices, our evil inclinations, selfishness, pride and sensuality. We perfectly understand how much the first of these aspects of our humanity need to be developed and strengthened, and how much instead the second ones must be overcome, combatted and transformed. In this way — in living contact with Jesus, in the contact of the disciple with the Master — there begins and develops the most sublime activity of man's work on himself that aims at the formation of his own humanity. In our lives we prepare ourselves to perform various activities in one or other profession; our interior task, on the other hand, tends solely to form the human person himself — that human person which is each one of us.

This task is the most personal collaboration with Jesus Christ, similar to that which occurred in his disciples when he called them to intimate friendship with him.

3.   Today's Gospel speaks of a banquet. We know that the Divine Master, calling us to collaborate with him — a collaboration which we as his disciples accept in order to become his apostles — invites us as he did at Cana of Galilee. In fact, he presents to us, as the Fathers of the Church have described in an expressive and symbolic way, two tables: one of the word of God, the other of the Eucharist. The work that we take on ourselves consists in approaching these two tables in order to be filled.

I know how many young people in Poland, boys and girls, who with joy, with trust, with an interior desire to know the truth and to find pure and beautiful love, approach the table of the word of God and the table of the Eucharist. On this occasion today I wish to emphasize the great significance of the various forms of that creative work which allows us to discover the deep value of life, the true attraction of youth, living in intimacy with Christ the Master, in his sanctifying grace. One discovers in this way that human life, on whose threshold youth still finds itself, has a rich meaning and that it is — always and everywhere — a free and conscious answer to the call of God, a well defined vocation.

4.   Some of you have discovered that Christ has called you in a particular way to his exclusive service, and that he wishes to see you at the altar as his ministers, or on the path of evangelical consecration through the religious vows. This discovery of a vocation is followed by a particular preparation of some years either in seminaries or in religious novitiates. These institutions --

worthy of praise in the life of the Church — never cease to attract young people who are ready to give themselves exclusively to the Redeemer, so that there is fulfilled what you so spontaneously sing: 'Come with me to save the world, it is already the twentieth century. . .'

Remember that I rejoice for every priestly and religious vocation, as a particular gift of Christ the Lord for the Church, for the People of God, as a singular witness of the Christian vitality of our dioceses, parishes, families. Here, today, with you, I entrust every young vocation to Our Lady of Jasna Góra and I offer it to her as a particular gift.

5.   During the banquet at Cana of Galilee, Mary asked the first sign from her Son on behalf of the young newlyweds and those in charge of the house. Mary does not cease to pray for you, for all the young people of Poland and of the whole world, so that there will be manifested in you the sign of a new presence of Christ in history.

And you, my dearest friends, remember well these words which the Mother of Christ spoke at Cana, turning to those who were to fill the water jars. She said then, pointing to her Son: 'Do whatever he tells you!' (Jn 2:5).

To you also she says the same thing today.

Accept these words.

Remember them.

Put them into practice.

THE HOMILY TO THE PRIESTS OF CZĘSTOCHOWA

Pope John Paul II held a meeting, in the
Cathedral of the Holy Family in
Częstochowa, of the diocesan clergy
and those belonging to the religious
orders. There, 'at the feet of the Mother
of God', he recalled similar encounters
with the clergy in Rome and in Mexico.
The Holy Father said:

1.   My dear brothers in the priesthood, and at the same time, in the same
priesthood of Christ, beloved sons,
     We meet here at the feet of the Mother of God, before the face of our
Mother: the Mother of priests. We meet in unusual circumstances, which you
certainly, like me, are deeply moved by. And yet this first Polish Pope who
today stands before you received the grace of a priestly vocation on Polish
soil, he passed through the Polish Major Seminary (for the most part when it
was underground, because it was during the Occupation); he studied at the
Theology Faculty of the Jagellonian University; he received priestly ordination
from the Polish bishop and inflexible prince of unforgettable memory,
Cardinal Adam Stefan Sapieha; and, with you, he shared in the same
experiences of the Church and the nation.
     This in particular I want to say to you at today's meeting. Everything
that was formed in me here, everything I have taken away from here, echoes
in all the meetings I have had with priests since 16 October 1978. And so
today, in this meeting with you, I wish especially to refer to the words that I
have said on those various occasions. In fact I believe that you all have some
share in their formation, and in part you have authorship rights. I also hold
that though these words have been already said in Rome or elsewhere, they
refer to you in Poland.

2.   Here is a part of the talk I gave to the diocesan and religious priests of
the Diocese of Rome last 9 November:
     I said: 'I remember the admirable, zealous and often heroic priests with
whom I was able to share the concern and the struggles . . . In my previous
episcopal work the Priests' Council rendered me great service, both as a
community and as a meeting-place for sharing, together with the Bishop,
common solicitude for the whole life of the presbyterium and for the
effectiveness of its pastoral activity . . . As I meet you here for the first time
and greet you with sincere affection,' I also said to the priests and religious of
Rome, 'I still have before my eyes and in my heart the presbyterium of the
Church in Cracow — all our meetings on various occasions — the many talks
that began right from the years in the Seminary — the meetings of priests —
ordination groups of the individual seminary courses, to which I always went
and in which I took part with joy and benefit!' (*L'Osservatore Romano*, 10
November 1978, p. 1, nos. 2–3).

3. And now let us return together to the great meeting with the Mexican priests at the Shrine of Our Lady of Guadalupe. I said these words to them:

'Servants of a great cause, on you largely depends the destiny of the Church in the spheres entrusted to your pastoral care. This imposes upon you the duty to have a deep awareness of the greatness of the mission that you have received, and an awareness of the need to make yourselves ever more fit for it. In fact, it is a question . . . of Christ's Church — what respect and love this ought to fill us with! — which you must serve with joy in holiness of life (cf. Eph 4:13). This lofty and demanding service cannot be rendered unless you have a clear and firmly-rooted conviction of your identity as priests of Christ, stewards and ministers of God's mysteries, instruments of salvation for people, witnesses to a kingdom that begins in this world but reaches fulfilment in the world to come' (nos. 2–3; *AAS* 71 (1979), p. 180).

4. Finally, the fourth enunciation, and perhaps the best known one: the Letter to all the priests of the Church on the occasion of Holy Thursday 1979. I felt the particularly strong need to address the priests of the whole Church precisely at the beginning of my pontificate. I wanted this to happen on the occasion of Holy Thursday, on the occasion of the 'feast of priests'. I had before my eyes that day in the Cathedral at Wawel, when we renewed together our faith in the priesthood of Jesus Christ and dedicated to him anew, at his complete disposal, our whole being, soul and body, so that he might be able to work through us and carry out his salvific work.

'Our pastoral activity demands,' I wrote, 'that we should be close to people and all their problems, whether these problems be personal, family or social ones, but it also demands that we should be close to all these problems "in a priestly way". Only then, in the sphere of all these problems, do we remain ourselves. Therefore if we are really of assistance in those human problems, and they are sometimes very difficult ones, then we keep our identity and are really faithful to our vocation. With great perspicacity we must seek, together with all men, truth and justice, the true and definitive dimensions of which we can only find in the Gospel, or rather in Christ himself' (no. 17: *AAS* 71 (1979), p. 404).

5. Dear Polish priests gathered today at Jasna Góra, those are the thoughts that I wanted to share with you. The priests of Poland have their own history, a history that has been written, in close connection with the history of the motherland, by the entire generations of the 'servants of Christ and stewards of the mysteries of God' (1 Cor 4:1) whom our land has given.

We have always felt a profound bond with the People of God, with this people from the midst of which we have been 'chosen', and for which we have been 'appointed' (cf. Heb 5:1). The witness of living faith that we draw from the Upper Room, from Gethsemane, from Calvary; from the faith that we absorbed with our mothers' milk; from the faith that was strengthened amid the hard trials suffered by our fellow-countrymen — this is our spiritual hallmark; the foundation of our priestly identity.

In today's meeting, could I fail to recall the thousands of Polish priests who lost their lives in the Last War, especially in the concentration camps?

But allow me to limit the memories that crowd·into my mind and heart.

I shall say only that this heritage of priestly faith, service and solidarity with the nation in her most difficult periods, which constitutes in a sense the foundation of the historical trust of society in the Polish priests, must always be developed by each of you and must, I would say, always be won again. Christ the Lord taught the Apostles what idea they were to have of themselves and what they were to demand of themselves: 'We are unworthy servants; we have only done what was our duty' (Lk 17:10). Dear brothers, Polish Priests, as you recall these words and the experiences of history, you must always keep before your eyes the demands arising from the Gospel that are the measure of your vocation. It is a great blessing, this trust that the Polish priest has to his credit with society when he is faithful to his mission and his attitude is clear and in keeping with the style developed by the Church in Poland in the last decades: namely, the style of the evangelical witness of social service. May God assist us in order that this style may not be exposed to any 'hesitation'.

Christ asks of his disciples that their light 'shine before men' (cf. Mt 5:16). We are well aware of the human weaknesses in each one of us. We think with humility of the trust that our Teacher and Redeemer has in us when he entrusts to our priestly hands the power over his body and his blood. I hope that, with the aid of his Mother, you will in these difficult and often unclear times be capable of behaving in such a way that 'your light may shine before men'. Let us pray for this without ceasing. Let us pray with great humility.

I also wish to express the earnest wish that Poland may not cease to be the motherland of priestly vocations and the land of the great witness given to Christ through the service of your lives: through the ministry of the word and of the Eucharist.

Love Mary, dear brothers! From that love do not cease to draw strength for your hearts. May she show herself for you and through you the Mother of all, who have such a great thirst for this motherhood.

Monstra te esse Matrem
Sumat per te preces
qui pro nobis natus
tulit esse tuus.

Amen.

THE ADDRESS TO THE MINERS AND WORKERS OF SILESIA

That afternoon, before leaving
Częstochowa, John Paul II held a Mass,
in the Monastery grounds at Jasna
Góra, attended by over a million miners
and workers from Upper Silesia and the
coalfields of Zagłębie. During the
ceremony he preached this sermon:

1.   Jasna Góra has become Poland's spiritual capital. Pilgrims come from
every part of our native soil, in order to find there unity with Christ the Lord
through the heart of his Mother. They come not only from Poland but also
from beyond her frontiers. The image of Our Lady of Jasna Góra has become
a sign of spiritual unity on the part of Poles throughout the world. It is also,
I would say, a sign by which to recognize our spirituality and also our place
in the great family of the Christian peoples gathered in the unity of the
Church. For wonderful is the reign of the Mother through her image in Jasna
Góra: the reign of the Heart, which is ever more necessary to the world,
which tends to express everything through cold calculations and purely
material ends.

I arrive at Jasna Góra as a pilgrim and I wish to unite myself cordially
with all belonging to this spiritual community, this great family spread over
the whole of the land of Poland and beyond her frontiers. I desire us all to
meet in the heart of the Mother. I join myself through faith, hope and prayer
with all those who cannot come here. I unite myself in particular with all the
communities of the Church of Christ in Poland, with all the diocesan
Churches and their Pastors, with all the parishes, with the religious families
of men and women.

In a special way I turn to you who have come here today from Silesia and
Zagłębie Dabrowskie. Both these lands, both these provinces of ancient and
modern Poland are dear to me. The wealth of present-day Poland is in great
part bound up with the natural resources with which Providence has endowed
these lands and with the great centres of human labour that have risen there
during the last centuries. Historically speaking, both Silesia and Zagłębie —
particularly Silesia — have always remained in close union with the see of
Saint Stanislaus. As former Metropolitan of Cracow, I wish to express my
special joy at this meeting between us today at the foot of Jasna Góra. I have
always been close in heart to the Church of Katowice, which contributes
special experiences and values to Catholic life in Poland as a whole.

2.   Chiefly the experience of immense work. The riches of the earth, both
those that appear on its surface and those that we must seek in its depths,
become riches for man only at the cost of human labour. This work, in its
many forms, both intellectual and manual, is necessary for man to fulfil the
magnificent mission that the Creator has entrusted to him, the mission
expressed in the book of Genesis with the words 'Subdue (the earth) and have

106

dominion' (Gen 1:28). The earth is entrusted to man, and through work man has dominion over it.

Work is also the fundamental dimension of man's life on earth. Work has for man a significance that is not merely technical but ethical. It can be said that man 'subdues' the earth when by his behaviour he becomes its master, not its slave, and also the master and not the slave of work.

Work must help man to become better, more mature spiritually, more responsible, in order that he may realize his vocation on earth both as an unrepeatable person and in community with others, especially in the fundamental human community constituted by the family. By joining together in this very community, whose character was established by the Creator himself from the beginning, a man and a woman give life to new human beings. Work must make it possible for this human community to find the means necessary for its formation and maintenance.

The reason for the family is one of the fundamental factors determining the economy of policy of work. These keep their ethical character, when they take into consideration the needs and the rights of the family. Through work the adult human being must earn the means needed to maintain his family. Motherhood must be treated in work policy and economy as a great end and a great task in itself. For with it is connected the mother's work in giving birth, feeding and bringing up, and no one can take her place. Nothing can take the place of the heart of a mother always present and always waiting in the home. True respect for work brings with it due esteem for motherhood. It cannot be otherwise. The moral health of the whole of society depends on that.

My thoughts and my heart open again to you, hard-working people, with whom I have been linked in various ways by my personal life and my pastoral ministry. I wish your work not to cease to be the source of your social strength. Thanks to your work, may your homes be strong. Thanks to your work, may the whole of our motherland be strong.

3. Therefore I turn my gaze once more to the industrious Silesia and Zagłebie, towards the blast-furnaces and chimneys of the factories: it is a land of great work and of great prayer. These two are linked closely together in the tradition of this People, whose usual greeting is given with the words *Szczęść Boże* (May God give you his help), words that link the thought of God to human work, referring one to the other.

It is right that I should bless Divine Providence today, giving thanks for the fact that the immense development of industry – the development of human work – has gone hand in hand with the building of churches, the erection of parishes and the deepening and strengthening of faith. For the fact that development has not implied de-Christianization, the rupture of the alliance that must be set up in the human soul between work and prayer, in keeping with the motto of the Benedictines: *Ora et labora.* In every human work prayer sets up a reference to God the Creator and Redeemer and it also contributes to complete 'humanization' of work. 'Work exists . . . for resurrection' (C. K. Norwid). Man, indeed, is by his Creator's will called from the beginning to subdue the earth by his work and also has been created in the image and after the likeness of God himself. There is no other way for him to find himself and confirm who he is except by seeking God in prayer. By seeking God, by meeting him in prayer, man is bound to find himself, since he is like God. He cannot find himself except in his Prototype. He cannot confirm his 'dominion' over the earth by work except by praying at the same time.

Dear brothers and sisters, hard-working people of Silesia, Zagłebie and the whole of Poland, do not let yourselves be seduced by the temptation to think that man can fully find himself by denying God, erasing prayer from his life and remaining only a worker, deluding himself that what he produces can on its own fill the needs of the human heart. 'Man shall not live by bread alone' (Mt 4:4). This was said by him who knows the human heart and has given sufficient proof of caring for material needs. The Lord's Prayer includes an invocation for bread, but man shall not live by bread alone. Remain faithful to the experience of the generations that have cultivated this earth and brought its hidden treasures to the surface with God in their hearts and a prayer on their lips. Keep what has been the source of strength for your fathers and forefathers, for your families and for your communities. Let 'prayer and work' become a fresh fountain of strength in this generation and also in the hearts of your children, your grandchildren and great-grandchildren.

4.   I say to you: *Szcześć Boze* — May God give you his help.

I say this prayer through the Heart of the Mother, the Heart of her whose reign in Jasna Góra consists in being a loving Mother for all of us.

I say this prayer through the Heart of that Mother who chose for herself a place closer to your homes, your mines and factories, your villages and cities, the place called Piekary. Put what I say to you today from this height of Jasna Góra beside what I have so often said to you, as Metropolitan of Cracow, from the height of Piekary. And remember it.

Amen.

Szcześź Boze — May God give you his help.

Amen.

THE FAREWELL TO JASNA GÓRA

In conformity with the tradition of a
farewell visit to the Sanctuary by every
pilgrim to Jasna Góra, the Pope
returned to the monastery before his
departure for Cracow during the
afternoon of 6 June. He prayed once
again before the image of the Patroness
of Poland. He reaffirmed his
commitment of consecration to the
Mother of the Church as follows:

Our Lady of Jasna Góra!

1.   There is a custom — a beautiful custom — for pilgrims whom you have
welcomed at Jasna Góra to make a farewell visit to you before leaving here. I
remember very many of these farewell visits, these special audiences that you,
Mother of Jasna Góra, have granted me, when I was still a high-school
student and came here with my Father and the pilgrimage from the whole of
my native parish of Wadowice. I remember the audience that you granted to
me and to my companions when we came here clandestinely, as
representatives of the university students of Cracow, during the terrible
Occupation, in order not to interrupt the continuity of the university
pilgrimages to Jasna Góra, pilgrimages begun in the memorable year 1936. I
remember so many other farewell visits to you, so many other moments of
parting, when I came here as chaplain to young people, later as Bishop,
leading pilgrimages of priests from the Archdiocese of Cracow.

2.   Today I have come to you, Our Lady of Jasna Góra, with the venerable
Primate of Poland, with the Archbishop of Cracow, with the Bishop of
Czestochowa and with the whole of the Episcopate of my motherland, to bid
you farewell once more and to ask your blessing for my journey. I come here,
after these days that I have spent with them — as the first servant of your Son
and as the successor of Peter in the See of Rome. The meaning of this
pilgrimage is quite inexpressible. I shall not even try to find the words to
express what it has been for me and for us all, and what it will never cease to
be. And so, Mother of the Church and Queen of Poland, forgive us all if we
thank you only with the silence of our hearts; and if with this silence we sing
you our 'preface' of farewell.

3.   I just wish, in your presence, to thank once more my beloved brothers in
the Episcopate: the Cardinal Primate, the Archbishops and Bishops of the
Church in Poland, from the circle of whom I have been called, and with
whom I have been profoundly linked from the beginning and continue to be
so. Here are those who becoming, in Saint Peter's words, models of the flock
(*forma gregis*) (cf. 1 Pet 5:3) with all their hearts serve the Church and the
motherland, without sparing their energies. Venerable Brothers, I wish to
thank all of you, and in a special way you, the Eminent and beloved Primate

of Poland, repeating once more (perhaps also without words) what I have already said in Rome on 22 and 23 October of last year. Today I repeat the same things — with my thoughts and with my heart — here, in the presence of Our Lady of Jasna Góra.

I express my cordial thanks to all who have been pilgrims with me here during these days — in particular the custodians of the Shrine, the Pauline Fathers, led by their Superior General and Guardian of Jasna Góra.

4.   Our Lady of the Bright Mountain, Mother of the Church! Once more I consecrate myself to you 'in your maternal slavery of love'. *Totus tuus!* — I am all yours! I consecrate to you the whole Church — everywhere and to the ends of the earth! I consecrate to you Humanity; I consecrate to you all men and women, my brothers and sisters. All the Peoples and the Nations. I consecrate to you Europe and all the continents. I consecrate to you Rome and Poland, united, through your servant, by a fresh bond of love.

Mother, accept us!

Mother, do not abandon us!

Mother, be our guide!

THE ARRIVAL IN CRACOW BY HELICOPTER

John Paul II travelled to Cracow in a helicopter. Many thousands of the faithful were waiting for him in a meadow in the centre of the city notwithstanding the heavy rain which was falling. In greeting 'my beloved Cracow as a pilgrim', the Holy Father said:

Beloved brothers and sisters!

By the inscrutable design of Providence I had to leave the episcopal see of Saint Stanislaus at Cracow and from 16 October 1978 to occupy that of Saint Peter in Rome. The choice of the Sacred College was for me an expression of the will of Christ himself. To this will I desire to remain always submissive and faithful. I desire furthermore to serve, with all my strength, the great cause to which I was called, that is, the proclaiming of the Gospel and the work of salvation. I thank you because you have helped me spiritually, above all with your prayers.

If I say this with the first words with which I greet you, it is because Christ writes his calls in the living heart of man. And my heart was and has not ceased to be united with you, with this city, with this patrimony, with this 'Polish Rome'.

Here, in this land, I was born.

Here, in Cracow, I spent the greater part of my life, beginning with my enrolment in the Jagellonian University in 1938.

Here, I received the grace of my priestly vocation.

I was consecrated Bishop in the Cathedral of Wawel, and in January 1964 I inherited the great patrimony of the Bishops of Cracow.

Cracow, from the tenderest years of my life, has been for me a particular synthesis of all that it means to be Polish and Christian. She has always spoken of the great historic past of my Motherland. She always represented for me in a sublime way the spirit of my country.

I remember the old Cracow of the university years of my youth – and the new Cracow which with the constitution of Nowa Huta has almost tripled in size. This Cracow, in whose problems I participated as pastor, as Bishop, as Cardinal.

Today, I greet my beloved Cracow as a pilgrim.

I greet all that which constitutes it: the witness of history, the tradition of the kings, the cultural and scientific patrimony and, at the same time, the modern metropolis.

I especially greet you, the residents of Cracow, all of you and each one of you. I come back to you for the few days of the jubilee of Saint Stanislaus, as to a great family.

You are so close to me. Because of the separation to which the Lord has called me, I feel even closer to you. I wish to express my sentiments and good wishes with the words of Saint Ignatius of Antioch. 'May the grace of the Lord now give you everything in abundance . . . Just as you have comforted me in every way, so may the Lord Jesus give you consolation. You have shown me your love both when I was present and when I was absent; may the Lord reward you for this' (Letter to the faithful of Smyrna, IX, 2: *Sources Chrétiennes X*, 164).

During these few days that I will be spending with you I wish to do the same things that I have always done: proclaim 'the great works of God' (Acts 2:11), give witness to the Gospel and serve the dignity of man. As Saint Stanislaus did so many centuries ago.

IN THE CATHEDRAL OF CRACOW

After his arrival in Cracow, John Paul II went to the Tomb of St Stanislaus in the city's Cathedral where he listened to a brief message of welcome and homage from the Archbishop, Monsignor Franciszek Macharski. The Pope replied, with a greeting to his 'beloved archdiocese', as follows:

After arriving in Cracow, I have directed my first steps to the Cathedral, in order to meet you who were waiting here at the tomb of Saint Stanislaus, of the blessed Queen Hedwig and of our kings, of our military commanders, and of our inspired national poets. You all know very well what this Wawel Cathedral has been and is for me.

I greet the whole of the well-loved presbyterium of the Church of Cracow, gathered around the relics of its Patron, its Bishop of nine centuries ago, and also with his successor of the present day, the Metropolitan of Cracow, and his brothers in the Episcopate.

I greet you all.

Since 1972 I prepared, together with you, my dear Brothers, this Jubilee that I am now celebrating with you, although it is in a way different from what I expected. Inscrutable are the designs of God! Inscrutable his ways!

We planned together that during this year visits should be made in all the parishes of the Archdiocese of Cracow with the relics of Saint Stanislaus, and I know that this plan is being carried out. I would like to add to this series of visits my own present visit in the Wawel basilica, which, as the Cathedral, is the mother church of all the churches and parishes of the Archdiocese. Through my visit to the holy relics here in the Cathedral I am indirectly visiting every parish. In this way I am also visiting each one of you, dear brothers and sons, each one in his place of work. I am visiting all the communities of the People of God of which you are the pastors. Please greet for me your parishes, your churches, your chapels. Greet all the shrines, which are always so dear to my heart.

Greet the families, the parents, the young people.

Now, as then, I pray every day for my beloved Archdiocese

for the families;

for the parishes and deaneries;

for the Religious Congregations of men and women;

for the Cracow Seminary and all the Seminaries situated in the City;

for the Theological Athenaeum, heir to the most ancient Faculty in Poland, belonging to the Jagellonian University, which we owe to the Blessed Queen Hedwig;

for the Council of Priests;

for the Metropolitan Chancery;

for the Chapter responsible for the care of Wawel;

for the Synod of the Archdiocese and metropolis.

Blessed be the God and Father of Our Lord Jesus Christ, who has blessed us with the gift of a special unity in his service. Amen.

. . . and from all war
deliver us, O Lord

Thursday 7 June

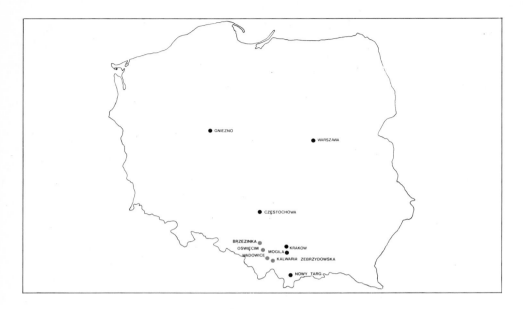

AT THE SANCTUARY OF KALWARIA ZEBRYDOWSKA

The sixth day of John Paul II's pilgrimage in Poland began, on the morning of Thursday 7 June, with a pilgrimage to the shrine of Our Lady of Kalwaria Zebrydowska. The Holy Father arrived from Cracow in a helicopter at about 9.45 a.m. In the course of a religious ceremony, which took place in the open, the Pope pronounced the following homily:

1.   I really do not know how to thank Divine Providence for granting me to revisit this place: Kalwaria Zebrzydowska, the Shrine of the Mother of God, the holy places of Jerusalem connected with the life of Jesus and that of his Mother reproduced here, the 'little ways', as they are called. I visited them often as a boy and as a young man. I visited them as a priest. Especially, I often visited the Shrine of Kalwaria as Archbishop of Cracow and Cardinal. Many times we came here, the priests and I, to concelebrate before the Mother of God. We came in the yearly pilgrimage in August and in the pilgrimage of certain groups in the spring and the autumn. More frequently however I came here alone and, walking along the little ways of Jesus Christ and his Mother, I was able to meditate on their holy mysteries and

recommend to Christ through Mary the specially difficult and uniquely responsible problems in the complexity of my ministry. I can say that almost none of these problems reached its maturity except here, through ardent prayer before the great mystery of faith that Kalwaria holds within itself.

It is a mystery with which you are all quite familiar, you the Bernardine (Franciscan) Fathers and Brothers who are guardians of this Shrine, you the people who live here, who are members of the parish, and you the many, many pilgrims who come here at different times and in various groups from all over Poland, especially from the area close to the Carpathians, from both sides of the Tatra, some of you coming several times. Kalwaria has something in it that attracts a person. What produces this effect? Perhaps part of it is the natural beauty of the landscape extending to the foot of the Polish Beskid Mountains. It certainly reminds us of Mary going into the hill country to visit Elizabeth (Lk 1:39). But what chiefly draws a person here again and again is the mystery of the union of the Mother with the Son and of the Son with the Mother. This mystery is recounted in abundant artistic fashion by all the chapels and little churches extending around the central Basilica reigned over by the image of Our Lady of Kalwaria, which was crowned with the diadem of Pope Leo XIII on 15 August 1887 by Cardinal Albin Dunajewski. For the centenary of the act, which will take place in 1987, you will prepare yourselves during the coming nine years. May these be years of deeply lived preparation by you and may they bring you still closer to the mysteries of the Mother and the Son, which have been so strongly lived and meditated upon in this holy place.

The mystery of the union of the Mother with the Son and of the Son with the Mother on the Way of the Cross and the path of her funeral from the Chapel of the Dormition to the Tomb of Our Lady. Finally, the mystery of their union in glory, recalled by the little ways of the Assumption and the Coronation. The whole of this, well laid out in time and space and covered with the prayers of so many hearts, of so many generations, constitutes a unique living treasury of the faith, hope and charity of the People of God in this land. Every time that I came here I was aware of drawing from that treasury. And I was always aware that the mysteries of Jesus and Mary on which we meditate while praying for the living and the dead are truly inscrutable. We keep coming back to them, and each time we encourage ourselves to return here again and again in order to immerse ourselves in them. In these mysteries is expressed a synthesis of all that is part of our earthly pilgrimage, of all that is part of our 'little ways' of daily life. All of this was assumed by the Son of God, and through his Mother it is restored to man again: it is permeated by a new light, without which human life is senseless and remains in the darkness. 'He who follows me will not walk in darkness, but will have the light of life' (Jn 8:12). That is the fruit of my many years of pilgrimage through the little ways of Kalwaria. The fruit that I am sharing with you today.

3. What I want to give you courage and enthusiasm for is this: keep visiting this Shrine. Even more do I want to say this to all of you, but

especially to the young people (for it is the young who are particularly fond of this place): Keep praying; we 'ought always to pray and not lose heart' (Lk 18:1), as Jesus taught. Pray and through prayer shape your lives.

'Man shall not live by bread alone' (Mt 4:4), and it is not by the temporal alone nor merely by the satisfaction of material needs, by ambition, or by desire that man is man. 'Man shall not live by bread alone, but by every word that proceeds from the mouth of God' (Mt 4:4). To live by this Word, the Divine Word, we ought to pray 'and not lose heart'.

From this place I send to everyone who is listening to me here or anywhere this simple fundamental invitation from the Pope to pray.

It is the most important invitation.

It is the most essential message.

May the Shrine of Kalwaria continue to gather pilgrims, and to serve the Archdiocese of Cracow and the whole of the Church in Poland. May a great work of renewal be accomplished here for men, women, young people, liturgical service of the altar, and for everyone.

And I ask all those who will continue to come here to pray for one of the pilgrims of Kalwaria whom Christ has called with the same words that he spoke to Simon Peter: 'Feed my lambs . . . Feed my sheep' (Jn 21:15–19).

I ask you to pray for me here during my life and after my death.

Amen.

IN THE PARISH CHURCH OF WADOWICE

During the morning, John Paul II visited his birthplace, Wadowice. A service was held in the church where he was baptized, and the Pope addressed the citizens and the many pilgrims, who had arrived for the occasion, as follows:

Dear people of Wadowice,

It is with deep emotion that I arrive today in the town of my birth, in the parish in which I was baptized and accepted as part of the ecclesial community, and in the surroundings to which I was linked for eighteen years of my life, from when I was born to when I left school.

I want to thank you for greeting me, and also to greet and welcome all of you cordially. Many years have gone by since I lived in Wadowice and there have been changes. So I greet the new inhabitants of Wadowice, but I do so while thinking of the former inhabitants, that generation that lived its youth here in the period between the First World War and the Second. In mind and heart I go back to the elementary school in Rynek (Market Square) and to the Wadowice secondary school dedicated to Marcin Wadowita that I went to. In mind and heart I go back to those who grew up with me, the boys and girls who were with me in school, and to our parents and teachers. Some of those who grew up with me are still here and I greet them with special cordiality. Others are scattered throughout Poland and the world, but they too will come to know of this meeting between us.

We know how important are the first years of life, of childhood and of youth for the development of human personality and character. These are the very years that bind me inseparably to Wadowice, to the town and the area around it, to the River Skawa and the Beskid Range. For that reason I have wanted very much to come here, in order to thank God with you for all the blessings that I have received. My prayer is for so many people who have died, beginning with my parents, my brother and my sister, whose memory is linked for me with this city.

On the human level, I want to express my feelings of deep gratitude to Monsignor Edward Zacher, who was my religion teacher in the Wadowice secondary school, who later gave the talk at my first Mass and at my first celebrations as Bishop, Archbishop and Cardinal here in the church of Wadowice, and who finally has spoken again today on the occasion of this new stage in my life, which cannot be explained except by the boundless mercy of God and the exceptional protection of the Mother of God.

When in thought I look back over the long path of my life, I reflect on how the surroundings, the parish and my family brought me to the baptismal font of the church of Wadowice, where I was given on 20 June 1920 the grace to become a son of God, together with faith in my Redeemer. I have already solemnly kissed this font in the year of the Millennium of the

Baptism of Poland, when I was Archbishop of Cracow. Today I wish to kiss it again as Pope, successor of Saint Peter.

I wish to fix my gaze on the face of the Mother of Perpetual Help in her image at Wadowice.

I ask all of you to surround me with unceasing prayer before the image of this Mother.

IN THE CONCENTRATION CAMP AT OSWIECIM (AUSCHWITZ)

That same afternoon, the Holy Father
celebrated Mass in the concentration
camp at Oswiecim (Auschwitz) and
commemorated the martyrs of the
camps. He preached the following
sermon:

1.   'This is the victory that overcomes the world, our faith' (1 Jn 5:4).
    These words from the Letter of Saint John come to my mind and enter
my heart as I find myself in this place in which a special victory was won
through faith. Through the faith that gives rise to love of God and of one's
neighbour, the unique love, the supreme love that is ready to 'lay down
(one's) life for (one's) friends' (Jn 15:13; cf. 10:11). A victory therefore
through love enlivened by faith to the extreme point of the final definitive
witness.

    This victory through faith and love was won in this place by a man whose
first name is Maximilian Mary. Surname: Kolbe. Profession (as registered in
the books of the concentration camp): Catholic priest. Vocation: a son of Saint
Francis. Birth: a son of simple, hardworking, devout parents, who were
weavers near Łódź. By God's grace and the Church's judgment: Blessed.
    The victory through faith and love was won by him in this place, which
was built for the negation of faith – faith in God and faith in man – and to
trample radically not only on love but on all signs of human dignity, of
humanity. A place built on hatred and on contempt for man in the name of a
crazed ideology. A place built on cruelty. On the entrance gate which still
exists, is placed the inscription 'Arbeit macht frei,' which has a sardonic
sound, since its meaning was radically contradicted by what took place
within.

    In this site of the terrible slaughter that brought death to four million
people of different nations, Father Maximilian voluntarily offered himself for
death in the hunger bunker for a brother and so won a spiritual victory like
that of Christ himself. This brother still lives today in the land of Poland.
    But was Father Maximilian Kolbe the only one? Certainly he was a
victory that was immediately felt by his companions in captivity and is still
felt today by the Church and the world. However, there is no doubt that
many other similar victories were won. I am thinking, for example, of the
death in the gas chamber of a concentration camp of the Carmelite Sister
Benedicta of the Cross, whose name in the world was Edith Stein, who was
an illustrious pupil of Husserl and became one of the glories of contemporary

Germany philosophy, and who was a descendent of a Jewish family living in Wrockław.

Where the dignity of man was so horribly trampled on, victory was won through faith and love.

Can it still be a surprise to anyone that the Pope born and brought up in this land, the Pope who came to the see of Saint Peter from the diocese in whose territory is situated the camp of Oswiecim, should have begun his first Encyclical with the words 'Redemptor Hominis' and should have dedicated it

as a whole to the cause of man, to the dignity of man, to the threats to him, and finally to his inalienable rights that can so easily be trampled on and annihilated by his fellowmen? Is it enough to put man in a different uniform, arm him with the apparatus of violence? is it enough to impose on him an ideology in which human rights are subjected to the demands of the system, completely subjected to them, so as in practice not to exist at all?

2.   I am here today as a pilgrim. It is well known that I have been here many times. So many times! And many times I have gone down to Maximilian Kolbe's death cell and stopped in front of the execution wall and passed among the ruins of the cremation furnaces of Brzezinka. It was impossible for me not to come here as Pope.

I have come then to this special shrine, the birthplace, I can say, of the patron of our difficult century, just as nine centuries ago Skałka was the place of the birth under the sword of Saint Stanislaus, Patron of the Poles.

I have come to pray with all of you who have come here today and with the whole of Poland and the whole of Europe. Christ wishes that I who have become the Successor of Peter should give witness before the world to what constitutes the greatness and the ministry of contemporary man, to what is his defeat and his victory.

I have come and I kneel on this Golgotha of the modern world, on these tombs, largely nameless like the great tomb of the Unknown Soldier. I kneel before all the inscriptions that come one after another bearing the memory of the victims of Oswiecim in the languages: Polish, English, Bulgarian, Romany, Czech, Danish, French, Greek, Hebrew, Yiddish, Spanish, Flemish, Serbo-Croat, German, Norwegian, Russian, Romanian, Hungarian and Italian.

In particular I pause with you, dear participants in this encounter, before the inscription in Hebrew. This inscription awakens the memory of the People whose sons and daughters were intended for total extermination. This People draws its origin from Abraham, our father in faith (cf. Rom 4:12), as was expressed by Paul of Tarsus. The very people that received from God the commandment 'Thou shalt not kill' itself experienced in a special measure what is meant by killing. It is not permissible for anyone to pass by this inscription with indifference.

Finally, the last inscription: that in Polish. Six million Poles lost their lives during the second world war: a fifth of the nation. Yet another stage in the centuries-old fight of this nation, my nation, for its fundamental rights among the peoples of Europe. Yet another loud cry for the right to a place of its own on the map of Europe. Yet another painful reckoning with the conscience of mankind.

3. 'Oswiecim is such a reckoning. It is impossible merely to visit it. It is necessary on this occasion to think with fear of how far hatred can go, how far man's destruction of man can go, how far cruelty can go.

Oswiecim is a testimony of war. War brings with it a disproportionate growth of hatred, destruction and cruelty. It cannot be denied that it also manifests new capabilities of human courage, heroism and patriotism, but the fact remains that it is the reckoning of the losses that prevails. That reckoning prevails more and more, since each day sees an increase in the destructive capacity of the weapons invented by modern technology. Not only those who directly bring wars about are responsible for them, but also those who fail to do all they can to prevent them. Therefore I would like to repeat in this place the words that Paul VI pronounced before the United Nations Organization:

'It is enough to remember that the blood of millions of men, numberless and unprecedented sufferings, useless slaughter and frightful ruin are the sanction of the covenant which unites you in a solemn pledge which must change the future history of the world: No more war, war never again. It is peace, peace which must guide the destinies of peoples and of all mankind' (*AAS* 57, 1965, p. 881).

If however Oswiecim's great call and the cry of man tortured here is to bear fruit for Europe, and for the world also, the Declaration of Human Rights must have all its just consequences drawn from it, as John XXIII urged in the encyclical Pacem in Terris. For the Declaration is 'a solemn recognition of the personal dignity of every human being; as assertion of everyone's right to be free to seek out the truth, to follow moral principles, discharge the duties imposed by justice, and lead a fully human life. It also recognized other rights connected with these' (John XXIII, *Pacem in Terris*, IV – *AAS* 55, 1963, pp. 295–296). There must be a return to the wisdom of the old Teacher Paweł Włodkowic, Rector of the Jagellonian University at Cracow and the rights of nations must be ensured: their right to existence, to freedom, to independence, to their own culture, and to honourable development. Włodkowic wrote: 'Where power is more at work than love, people seek their own interests and not those of Jesus Christ and accordingly they easily depart from the rule of God's law . . . All the kinds of law are against those who threaten people wishing to live in peace: against them is the civil law . . . the canon law . . . the natural law, expressed in the principle 'Do to others what you would have done to you.' Against them is the divine law, in that . . . the commandment 'Thou shalt not steal' forbids all robbery and the commandment 'Thou shalt not kill' forbids all violence' (Paweł Włodkowic, *Saevientibus* (1415), *Tract*. II, *Solutio quaest*. 4a; cf. L. Ehrlich, *Pisma wybrane Pawla Włodkowica*, Warszawa 1968, t. l, s. 61; 58–59).

Never one at the other's expense, at the cost of the enslavement of the other, at the cost of conquest, outrage, exploitation and death.

He who is speaking these words is the successor of John XXIII and Paul VI. But he is also the son of a nation that in its history has suffered many afflictions from others. He says this, not to accuse but to remind. He is speaking in the name of all the nations whose rights are being violated and forgotten. He is saying it because he is urged to do so by the truth and by solicitude for man.

4. Holy is God! Holy and strong! Holy immortal One,
    From plague, from famine, from fire and from war
    and from war, deliver us, Lord.
    Amen.

Learn to know Christ
and make yourselves
known by Him

Friday 8 June

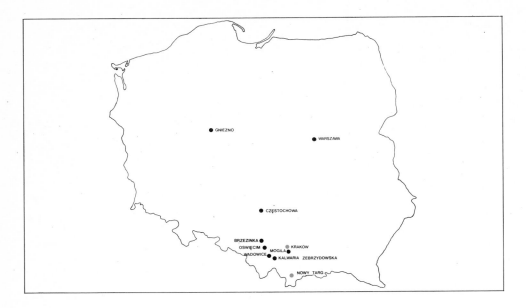

THE SERMON DURING THE MASS AT NOWY TARG

On the morning of Friday 8 June in front of the image of Our Lady Queen of Podhale which had been brought from the Sanctuary of Ludźmierz, John Paul II was present at the celebration of a Mass. Already in the early hours, thousands of the faithful had gathered on the airfield of Nowy Targ. The Holy Father arrived by helicopter from Cracow at 10.15 a.m. The Pope preached the sermon.

1. 'From the Baltic Sea to the mountain peaks . . .'
   To the peaks of the Tatra.
   In my pilgrimage through Poland, I have occasion today to come near to those mountains, the Tatra Mountains, that for centuries have constituted the southern frontier of Poland. This has been the most closed and most shielded frontier, and at the same time the most open and friendly one. Across this frontier passed the roads towards neighbours, towards like cultures. Even during the last occupation these roads were the ones most often taken by the refugees going south, trying to reach the Polish army, which was fighting for the freedom of the homeland beyond its borders.

With all my heart I wish to greet these places to which I have always been so closely bound. I also wish to greet all those who have come here, both from Podhale and from the lower Carpathians, from the Archdiocese of Cracow and from even further: from the Dioceses of Tarnow and Przemysl. Permit me to appeal to the ancient bond of being neighbours and to greet you all, just as I was accustomed to do when I was Metropolitan of Cracow.

2.   Here, in this place at Nowy Targ, I wish to speak of the Polish land, because here it shows itself particularly beautiful and rich in landscapes. Man needs the beauty of nature, and so it is not surprising that people come here from various parts of Poland and from abroad. They come both in summer and in winter. They seek rest. They want to find themselves again through contact with nature. They want to rebuild their energies through the wholesome physical exercise of walking, climbing and skiing. This hospital region is also a land of great pastoral work, because people come here to regain not only their physical strength but their spiritual strength too.

3.   This beautiful land is at the same time a difficult land. Rocky, mountainous. Not as fertile as the plain of the Vistula. And so permit me, precisely from this land of the lower Carpathians and the lower Tatra, to make reference to something that has always been very dear to the heart of the Poles: a love for the land and work in the fields. No-one can deny that this represents not only a feeling, an affective bond, but also a great social and economic problem. These parts are especially well acquainted with the problem, because it was precisely from these places, where there was the greatest lack of cultivable soil and sometimes great poverty, that people emigrated far away, beyond Poland, beyond the seas. There they sought work and bread, and they found it. Today I wish to say to all those people scattered throughout the world, wherever they may be: *Szcześć Boze* — May God give you his help! Let them not forget their country of origin, family, Church, prayer and everything they took from here. Because even though they had to emigrate for lack of material goods, yet they took with them from here a great spiritual heritage. Let them take care that while they become rich materally they do not become spiritually impoverished: neither they, nor their children, nor their grandchildren.

This is the great and fundamental, right of man: the right to work and the right to the land. Although economic development may take us in another direction, although one may value progress based upon industrialization, although the generation of today may leave en masse the land and agricultural work, still the right to the land does not cease to form the foundation of a sound economy and sociology.

During my visit it is only right that I offer some good wishes, and I therefore express to my native land my heartfelt wish that what has always constituted the strength of the Polish people — even during the most arduous periods of history — namely the personal bond with the land, may not cease to be so even in our industrialized generation. Hold in great esteem the work of

the fields; appreciate it and value it! And may Poland never want for bread and food!

4. This good wish is united to another. The Creator has given the earth to man so that 'He may subject' it — and upon this dominion of man over the earth he based man's fundamental right to life. This right is closely bound up with man's vocation to family life and to procreation. 'This is why a man leaves his father and mother and joins himself to his wife, and they will become one flesh' (Gen 2:24). Just as the earth, by the providential decree of the Creator, bears fruit, so too this union in the love of two persons: man and woman, bears fruit in a new human life. Of this lifegiving unity of persons the Creator made the first sacrament, and the Redeemer confirmed this never-ending sacrament of love and of life, giving it a new dignity and impressing on it the seal of its holiness. Man's right to life is linked, by the will of the Creator and in virtue of the Cross of Christ, to the indissoluble sacrament of Matrimony.

And so, beloved fellow-countrymen, on this visit of mine I express the wish that this sacred right may not cease to form the life of the Polish land; both here, in the lower Tatra, in the lower Carpathians, and everywhere. It is rightly said that the family is the fundamental cell of social life. It is the fundamental human community. As goes the family, so goes the nation, because such is man. So I express the wish that you may be strong, thanks to families deeply rooted in the strength of God, and I express the wish that man may be able to develop fully on the basis of the indissoluble bond of spouses who are parents, in the family atmosphere that nothing can replace. Again I express the wish and I always pray for this, that the Polish family may beget life and may be faithful to the sacred right to life. If man's right to life is violated at the moment in which he is first conceived in his mother's womb, an indirect blow is struck also at the whole of the moral order, which serves to ensure the inviolable goods of man. Among those goods life occupies the first place. The Church defends the right to life, not only in regard to the majesty of the Creator, who is the First Giver of this life, but also in respect to the essential good of man.

5. I also wish to speak to the young people, who love these places in a special way and seek here not only physical but also spiritual rest. 'To rest,' once wrote Norwid, 'means "to begin anew" ' [a play on words in Polish]. Man's spiritual rest, as many groups of young people correctly realize, must lead to discovering and working out in oneself that 'new creature' that Saint Paul speaks of. To this end leads the path of the word of God, read and celebrated with faith and love, participation in the Sacraments, and especially in the Eucharist. To this end leads the way of understanding and realization of community, that is, the communion with people that stems from Eucharistic Communion, and also the understanding and realization of evangelical service, that is, of diaconia, Dear friends, do not give up that noble effort that enables you to become witnesses to Christ. A witness, in biblical language, means 'martyr'.

I entrust you to the Immaculate Virgin, to whom Blessed Maximilian Kolbe continually entrusted the whole world.

I entrust everyone to the Mother of Christ who reigns not far from here as Mother in her shrine at Ludzmierz, and also in that shrine that rises in the heart of the Tatra at Rusinowa Polana (how much the Servant of God, Brother Albert, loved that place, how much he admired and loved it from his hermitage at Kalatowki), and in many other shrines built at the foot of the Carpathians, in the Dioceses of Tarnow and Przemysl — to the East and to the West. And in the whole of Poland.

May the heritage of the faith of Christ and of the moral order be guarded by Saint Stanislaus, Bishop and martyr, patron of the Poles, witnesses to Christ for so many centuries in our native land.

IN THE CATHEDRAL OF WAWEL FOR THE CLOSURE OF THE ARCHDIOCESAN SYNOD

That same afternoon John Paul II closed the Synod of the Archdiocese of Cracow with a High Mass in the city's Cathedral. The Synod had lasted seven years; seven years of work, prayer and communion with Cardinal Wojtyła as one of its principal animators. Now, as Pope, he had wanted to return for this important occasion. During the Mass John Paul II preached the sermon.

Beloved Metropolitan of Cracow,
Venerable Bishops,
Dearest brothers and sisters,

1.   Today the ardent desire of my heart is fulfilled. The Lord Jesus, who called me from the See of Saint Stanislaus, on the vigil of his ninth centenary, permits me to participate at the closing of the Synod of the Archdiocese of Cracow, a Synod that has always been bound, in my mind, to this great jubilee of our Church. All of you know this very well, because I have dealt with this theme many times, and so I have no need to repeat it today. Perhaps I would not even be capable of saying everything which, in relation to this Synod, has passed in my mind and in my heart — just what hopes and plans I have tied to it in this decisive period of the history of the Church and of the motherland.

The Synod has been connected, for me and for all of you, to the anniversary of the ninth centenary of the ministry of Saint Stanislaus, who for seven years was Bishop of Cracow. The work programme thus foresaw a period from 8 May 1972 to 8 May 1979. During this whole time, we wanted to honour the Bishop and pastor (of nine centuries ago) of the Church in Cracow, and to try to express — according to our times and our contemporaries. Just as Saint Stanislaus of Szczepanow did it nine centuries ago, so too we want to do it nine centuries later. I am convinced that this way of honouring the memory of the great Patron of Poland is the most suitable. It corresponds both to the historical mission of Saint Stanislaus and to those great tasks facing today's Church and modern Christianity after the Second Vatican Council. The initiator of the Council, the Servant of God John XXIII, specified this task with the word *aggiornamento*. The aim of the work of seven years of the Synod of Cracow — in response to the essential goals of Vatican II — was to be the *aggiornamento* of the Church of Cracow, the renewal of the understanding of its salvific mission, as well as the exact programme for its accomplishment.

2.   The path that has led to this end has been marked out by the tradition of particular synods of the Church; suffice it to recall the two preceding

138

synods during the ministry of Cardinal Adam Stefan Sapieha. The rules for conducting the synodal activity were laid out by the Code of Canon Law. However, we have taken into consideration the fact that the teaching of the Second Vatican Council opens new perspectives here and, I would say, creates new tasks. If the Synod was to serve the realization of the teaching of Vatican II, it was to do so above all with the same idea and with the same system of work. This explains the whole plan of the pastoral Synod and its subsequent realization. One can say that for the formulation of the resolutions and of the documents, we have travelled over a longer, but a more complete path. This path has passed through the activity of hundreds of synodal study groups, in which large numbers of the faithful of the Church of Cracow have been able to express themselves. These groups, as is well-known, were in the greater part made up of Catholic lay people, who have had on the one hand the opportunity to penetrate deeply into the teaching of the Council, and on the other hand to express in this regard their own experiences, their own proposals that manifested their love for the Church, their sense of responsibility for the whole of the Church's life in the Archdiocese of Cracow.

During the preparatory stage of the final documents of the Synod, the study groups became centres where extensive consultations took place; in fact, the General Commission that co-ordinated the activity of all the working commissions turned to them, as did the commissions of experts that had been summoned right from the beginning of the Synod. In this way, those matters matured, which the Synod, linking itself again to the teaching of the Council, wished to transfer into the life of the Church of Cracow. It wished to form, in accordance with those matters, the future of the Church.

3.   Today, all that work, this journey of seven years, is already behind you. I never thought that at the close of the work of the Synod of Cracow I would take part as a guest coming from Rome. But if such is the will of God, permit me, at this time, to assume once again the role of that Metropolitan of Cracow who through the Synod had wished to pay back the great debt which he had contracted towards the Council, towards the universal Church, towards the Holy Spirit. Permit me also in this role – as I have said – to thank all the people who have built up this Synod, year after year, month after month, by their work, by their advice, by their creative contributions, by their zeal. In a way, my gratitude goes to the whole community of the People of God of the Archdiocese of Cracow, both ecclesiastics and laity: to the priests, to the men and women religious. Especially to all here present: to the Bishops, headed by my venerated successor as the Metropolitan of Cracow; in a particular way to Bishop Stanisław Smolenski, who as chairman of the General Commission has directed the work of the Synod. To all the members of the Commission, and once again to the Preparatory Commission, which in 1971 and 1972, under the direction of Monsignor Prof. E. Florkowski, prepared the constitution, the regulations and the programme of the Synod. To the Working Commissions, the Commissions of Experts, to the tireless Secretariat, to the Editorial Groups, and finally to all the Study Groups.

In this circumstance, perhaps I ought to have spoken differently, but it is

not possible for me. I have been too personally connected with this work.

I wish, then, in the name of all of you, to lay this finished work before the sarcophagus of Saint Stanislaus, in the centre of the Cathedral of Wawel; the work had in fact been undertaken in view of his jubilee.

And together with all of you I ask the Most Holy Trinity that this work may bear fruit a hundredfold.   Amen.

WITH THE UNIVERSITY STUDENTS IN CRACOW

The Holy Father had a very cordial meeting with the University students of Cracow. Before making the speech which is published here, he had a long and spontaneous and friendly dialogue with the students, answering questions and, in response to their remarks and their songs, improvising words of encouragement and affection which impressed and delighted his audience.

Dear young friends,

1.   Allow me to begin with my recollections, since it is still only a short time ago that I used to meet you regularly in the many pastoral centres for the university students of Cracow. We saw each other on various occasions and I think that we understood each other well. I shall never forget our exchange of Christmas good wishes with the shared Eucharist, the Advent and Lenten spiritual exercises and our other meetings.

This year I had to spend Lent in Rome and for the first time I spoke not to the Polish university students of Cracow but to the Roman university students. I shall quote you some passages of what I said to them in the Basilica of Saint Peter:

'Christ is . . . the One who made a radical change in the ways of understanding life. He showed that life is a passing over, not only to the limit of death, but to a new life. Thus the Cross became for us the supreme Chair of the truth of God and of man. We must all be pupils – no matter what our age is – of this Chair. Then we will understand that the Cross is also the cradle of the new man.

'Those who are its pupils look at life in this way, perceive it in this way. And they teach it in this way to others. They imprint this meaning of life on the whole of temporal reality: on morality, creativity, culture, politics, economics. It has very often been affirmed – as, for example, the followers of Epicurus sustained in ancient times, and as some followers of Marx do in our times for other reasons – that this concept of life distracts man from temporal reality and that it cancels it in a certain sense. The truth is quite different. Only this conception of life gives full importance to all the problems of temporal reality. It opens the possibility of placing them fully in man's existence. And one thing is certain: this conception of life does not permit shutting man up in temporary things, it does not permit subordinating him completely to them. It decides his freedom.

'Giving human life this "paschal" meaning, that is, that it is a passing over, a passing over to freedom, Jesus Christ taught with his word and even more with his own example that it is a test . . . the test of thought, of the "heart" and of the will, the test of truth and love. In this sense, it is at the same time the test of the Covenant with God . . .

'The concept of "test" is closely connected with the concept of responsibility. Both are addressed to our will, to our acts. Accept, dear friends, both these concepts — or rather both realities — as elements of the construction of one's own humanity. Thus humanity of yours is already mature and, at the same time, is still young. It is the phrase of the definitive formation of one's life project. This formation takes place particularly in the "academic" years, in the time of higher studies . . .

'It is necessary to undertake this test with all responsibility. It is at the same time a personal responsibility — for my life, for its future pattern, for its value — and also a social responsibility, for justice and peace, for the moral order of one's own native environment and of the whole of society. It is a responsibility for the real common good. A man who has such an awareness of the meaning of life does not destroy, but constructs the future. Christ teaches us this.'

After the evening I spent with the youth of Rome, during which nearly all received their Easter communion, I thought to myself: How alike students are everywhere! Everywhere they listen to the Word of God and participate in the liturgy with the same attention. I then thought of you, of the spiritual retreats of the Polish university students of Cracow, of the similar moment of recollection, reflection and living the silence in the Church of Saint Ann, or in that of the Mother of God at Nowa Wies, or in that of the Dominicans or of the Jesuits, during like encounters.

2.   I thought of you also in Mexico, when I met the local university students in the shrine of Our Lady of Guadalupe: Allow me to quote also some phrases from the letter that after my return from Mexico I wrote specially to the university students of Latin America:

'During my meeting with you I saw that you feel very deeply the evil that weighs upon the social life of the nations whose sons and daughters you are. You are troubled by the need of change, the need to build a better world, one that is more just and also more worthy of man. In this matter your desires coincide with the outlook that has become more and more marked through the teaching and apostolate of the present-day Church. The Second Vatican Council often responds to this aspiration to make life on earth more human, more worthy of man. This basically has reference to each human being and so to all human beings. It cannot lead to restrictions, exploitation, falsification or discrimination of any kind. It must bring with it the full truth concerning man and lead to full actualization of human rights. The correct actualization of this noble inspiration beating in the heart and will of the young requires that man be seen in the whole of his human dimension. Man must not be reduced to the sphere of his merely material needs.

144

Progress cannot be measured and should not be measured by economic categories alone. The spiritual dimension of the human being must be given its right place.

'Man is himself through the maturity of his spirit, his conscience and his relationship with God and neighbour.

'There will be no better world, no better arrangement of social life, unless preference is first given to the values of the human spirit. Remember this well, you who are justly longing for changes bringing a better and more just society, you who rightly oppose every kind of evil, of discrimination, of violence and of torture inflicted on human beings. Remember that the order that you desire is a moral order and you will not attain it in any way, if you do not give first place to all that constitutes the strength of the human spirit – justice, love and friendship' (*AAS* 71 (1979) 253–254).

3.   I rejoice today in meeting you again in the context of the jubilee of Saint Stanislaus in which I have the good fortune to participate. When we listen to the Gospel that the liturgy of the solemnity of Saint Stanislaus each year recalls to us, we see in our mind's eye Christ, the Good Shepherd, who 'lays down his life for the sheep' (Jn 10:11), who knows his own sheep and his own know him (cf. Jn 10:14), who goes after the lost sheep and, when he has found it, 'he lays it on his shoulders, rejoicing' (Lk 15:5), and brings it back with joy to the fold.

All that I can say to you is summed up in the words: Get to know Christ and make yourselves known to him. He knows each one of you in a particular way. It is not a knowledge that arouses opposition and rebellion, a knowledge that forces one to flee in order to safeguard his own inward mystery. It is not a knowledge made up of hypotheses and reducing man to his dimensions of social utility. The knowledge of Christ is a knowledge full of the simple truth about man and, above all, full of love. Submit yourselves to this simple and loving knowledge of the Good Shepherd. Be certain that he knows each one of you more than each one of you knows himself. He knows because he has laid down his life (cf. Jn 15:13).

Allow him to find you. A human being, a young person, at times gets lost in himself, in the world about him, and in all the network of human affairs that wrap him round. Allow Christ to find you. Let him know all about you and guide you. It is true that following someone requires also making demands on ourselves. That is the law of friendship. If we wish to travel together, we must pay attention to the road we are to take. If we go walking in the mountains, we must follow the signs. If we go mountain climbing, we cannot let go of the rope. We must also preserve our unity with the Divine Friend whose name is Jesus Christ. We must co-operate with him.

Many times I have spoken of this and have done so more amply and in greater detail than today. Remember, what I said before and am saying now, I said it and I am saying it from personal experience. I have always been amazed at the wonderful power that Christ holds over the human heart: he holds it not for just any reason or motive, not for any kind of career or profit, but only because he loves and lays down his life for his brethren (cf. Jn 15:13).

4.   You are the future of the world, of the nation, of the Church. 'Tomorrow depends on you.' Accept with a sense of responsibility the simple truth contained in this song of youth and ask Christ, through his Mother, that you may be able to face it.

You must carry into the future the whole of the experience of history that is called 'Poland'. It is a difficult experience, perhaps one of the most difficult in the world, in Europe, and in the Church. Do not be afraid of the toil; be afraid only of thoughtlessness and pusillanimity. From the difficult experience that we call 'Poland' a better future can be drawn, but only on condition that you are honourable, temperate, believing, free in spirit and strong in your convictions.

Be consistent in your faith.

Be faithful to the Mother of Fair Love. Have trust in her, as you shape your love and form your young families.

May Christ always be for you 'the way, and the truth, and the life'.

. . . through
his personal experience
as a worker . . .
the Pope has learned
the Gospel anew

Saturday 9 June

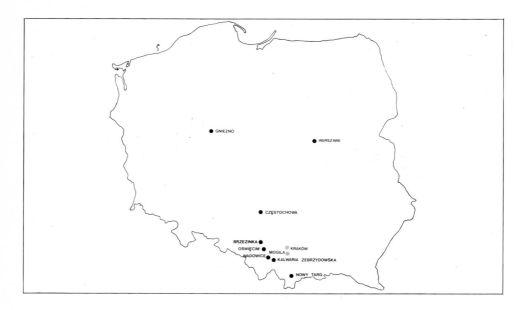

AT THE FACULTY OF THEOLOGY OF CRACOW

During an audience, which he gave to the students and alumni of the Faculty of Theology of Warsaw on the morning of 9 June, the Pope addressed them as follows:

Very Reverend and dear Dean,

Thank you for the invitation that enables me today to visit the Alma Mater that is so dear to me, where I was first a student and obtained my doctorate and later worked for many years as lecturer and professor.

Everyone knows my solicitude, when I was still Metropolitan of Cracow, to secure recognition for the rights due to this instutition, which has undoubtedly merited them, and to obtain full respect for its academic character in keeping with the needs of the present, which are different in nature and field of action from those of the past, from those, for instance, of the time when the Cracow Theological Faculty still belonged to the Jagellonian University.

1. In response to these needs, I endeavoured, during my ministry at Cracow,

first, to renew and increase the number of researchers and secure for them the qualifications that, in Church law (like the State procedure in Poland), constitute the basis of their autonomy; and

second, to secure for a large majority of theology students the basic academic teaching and the corresponding canonically valid academic degrees. This concerned in particular the students of the ecclesiastical seminaries (future priests and pastors) of the Archdiocese of Cracow and of the Dioceses of Czestochowa, Katowice and Tarnow, as well as the students belonging to the various religious orders and congregations, especially those studying at the Institute of the Vincentian Fathers in Cracow. This purpose was served by the system of agreements for scientific collaboration between the Papal Theological Faculty and the ecclesiastical seminaries that I have mentioned, which was approved by the Holy See (Sacred Congregation for Catholic Education). During the final year of my work in Cracow, preparatory talks had taken place for drawing up a similar agreement with the seminary of the Diocese of Kielce.

2.   The Theological Faculty, anxious to provide for the further instruction of priests and, in part, also of laypeople after they had completed their basic studies, has broadened the system of what are called studies akin to faculties of other kinds, such as catechetical, liturgical, and ascetical studies, studies for the theology of family pastoral care and the study of contemporary thought. These studies have their seat in Cracow. Apart from that, studies of a similar character are carried on at Rzeszow for the priests of the Diocese of Przemysl.

3.   The actvity I have been speaking of is part of the *cyclus institutionalis* (basic academic study). At the same time, the Theological Faculty, in conformity with its character and its statutes, also organizes the studies in the *cyclus specializationis*, preparing for the licentiate and doctorate. These studies are carried on principally in Cracow. Apart from that, an agreement has already been made with the Ordinary of Tarnow, to open a specialized Patrology Institute there. The Ecclesiological and Mariological Institute founded earlier at Czestochowa in agreement with the local Ordinary also has a specialized character. During my ministry the request was also sent on for the Pastoral Institute at Katowice.

4.   Specialization demands the singling out of the special scientific fields within which it is carried on, with the possibility of conferring academic degrees in accordance with the specialization. For that reason I asked Pope Paul VI, through the Sacred Congregation for Catholic Education, for the permission to confer scientific degrees not only in theology but also in philosophy.

Specialization in the field of Church history has a very particular reason for existing in Cracow, which has special resources providing possibilities in this field. Accordingly the Holy See will certainly go out to meet the requests for the approval of this specialization in the Cracow Athenaeum. The requests

have long since been forwarded, and as a result of them the Institute of Church History has sprung up at the Papal Theological Faculty.

Authorization for the setting up of that separate specialization, as well as the separate specialization of philosophy, corresponds fully with my first plans. This also concerns the philosophy specialization under the form of a third Faculty of the Cracow Athenaeum. I beg you to continue the activity along these lines.

I express my deep joy at being able today to do homage to the great past of our Alma Mater of Cracow before so venerable an audience, together with my Successor, and in the presence of the Bishops and the full Council of the Faculty. I wish to honour once again the Blessed Queen Hedwig, Foundress of the Cracow Theology Faculty. I also wish with all my heart and with full conviction to confirm the historic decision of my Predecessor Pope Boniface IX expressed in the Bull *Eximiae Devotionis Affectus* of 11 January 1397.

To the Athenaeum I love so much I wish the blessing of the Most Holy Trinity and the constant protection of Mary, Seat of Wisdom, as well as the faithful patronage of Saint John of Kety, who was a professor here more than five hundred years ago.

IN THE SANCTUARY OF THE HOLY CROSS AT MOGIŁA

The pilgrimage of the Holy Father in Poland is drawing to its close. On the morning of Saturday 9 June, John Paul II, who had been in Cracow since Wednesday night, said Mass at the Cistercian Abbey of Mogiła at Nowa Huta. The Pope preached the following sermon:

1.   Here I am again in front of this Cross, where I have so often come as a pilgrim, in front of the Cross that has remained as the most precious relic of our Redeemer for all of us.

When close to Cracow Nowa Huta was springing up, an enormous industrial complex and a new city, a new Cracow, it may not have been noticed that it was springing up beside this Cross, this relic that we have inherited with the ancient Cistercian abbey from the time of the Piasts. It was the year 1222, the time of Prince Leszek Biały, the time of Bishop Ivo Odrowąż, the period before the canonization of Saint Stanislaus. At that time, on the third centenary of our Baptism, the Cistercian abbey was founded here and the relic of the Holy Cross was then brought and has been for centuries the goal of pilgrimages from the Cracow area, from Kielce to the north, from Tarnów to the east, and from Silesia to the west. All this occurred in a place where tradition says there once stood Stara Huta, as it were the ancient historic mother of the present-day Nowa Huta.

I wish to greet here once more the pilgrims from Cracow, those from Silesia, and those from the Diocese of Kielce.

Let us go together, pilgrims, to the Lord's Cross. With it begins a new era in human history. This is the time of grace, the time of salvation. Through the Cross man has been able to understand the meaning of his own destiny, of his life on earth. He has discovered how much God has loved him. He has discovered, and he continues to discover by the light of faith, how great is his own worth. He has learnt to measure his own dignity by the measure of the Sacrifice that God offered in his Son for man's salvation: 'For God so loved the world that he gave his only Son, that whoever believes in him should not perish but have eternal life' (Jn 3:16).

Even if times change, even if what was once countryside near Cracow has given way to the emergence of a huge industrial complex, even if we are living in an age of dizzy advances in the natural sciences and equally amazing advances in technology, nevertheless the truth about the life of the human spirit, which is expressed by means of the Cross, knows no decline, is always relevant, never grows old. The history of Nowa Huta is also written by means of the Cross — first by means of the ancient Cross of Mogiła, the heritage of centuries, and then by means of the other Cross, the new one, which has been raised close by.

Where the Cross is raised, there is raised the sign that that place has now been reached by the Good News of man's salvation through Love. Where the cross is raised, there is the sign that evangelization has begun. Once our fathers raised the Cross in various places in the land of Poland as a sign that the Gospel had arrived there, that there had been a beginning of the evangelization that was to continue without break until today. It was with this thought also that the first Cross was raised in Mogiła, near Cracow, near Stara Huta.

The new wooden Cross was raised not far from here at the very time we were celebrating the Millennium. With it we were given a sign, that on the threshold of the new millennium, in these new times, these new conditions of life, the Gospel is again being proclaimed. A new evangelization has begun, as if it were a new proclamation, even if in reality it is the same as ever. The Cross stands high over the revolving world.

Today, before the Cross of Mogiła, the Cross of Nowa Huta, let us give thanks for the new beginning of evangelization that has been brought about here. And let us all pray that it may be as fruitful as the first evangelization — indeed, even more fruitful.

2. The new Cross that sprang up not far from the ancient relic of the Holy Cross in the Cistercian abbey proclaimed the birth of the new church. This birth is deeply engraved on my heart and, when I left the see of Saint Stanislaus for the see of Saint Peter, I took it with me as a new relic, a priceless relic of our time.

The new Cross appeared, when the land of the old countryside near Cracow that became the site of Nowa Huta saw the arrival of new men to begin new work. People did hard work here before that. They worked in the fields. The land was fertile and so they worked with pleasure. Some decades back industry began, great industry, heavy industry. People arrived here, coming from various places; they came to expend their energy here as workers in the iron industry.

It was they who brought with them the new Cross. It was they who raised it as a sign of their will to build a new church. This very Cross before which we are now standing. It was my good fortune, as your Archbishop and Cardinal, to bless and consecrate in 1977 this church that was born from a new Cross.

This church was born from the new work. I would make bold to say that it was born from Nowa Huta. For we all know that man's work bears deeply engraved on it the mystery of the Cross, the law of the Cross. In it comes true what the Creator said after the fall of man: 'In the sweat of your face you shall eat bread' (Gen 3:19). Both the old work in the fields, which makes wheat grow, but also thorns and thistles, and the new work in the blast-furnaces and the new foundries are always carried out 'with the sweat of one's brow'. The law of the Cross is engraved on man's work. It was with the sweat of his brow that the farmer worked. It is with the sweat of his brow that the iron-worker works. It is with the sweat of his brow — the terrible sweat of death — that Christ agonizes on the Cross.

The Cross cannot be separated from man's work. Christ cannot be separated from man's work. This has been confirmed here at Nowa Huta.

This has been the start of the new evangelization at the beginning of the new millennium of Christianity in Poland. We have lived this new beginning together and I took it with me from Cracow to Rome as a relic.

Christianity and the Church have no fear of the world of work. They have no fear of the system based on work. The Pope has no fear of men of work. They have always been particularly close to him. He has come from their midst. He has come from the quarries of Zakrzówek, from the Solvay furnaces in Borek Fałęcki, and then from Nowa Huta. Through all these surroundings, through his own experience of work, I make bold to say that the Pope learned the Gospel anew. He noticed and became convinced that the problems being raised today about human labour are deeply engraved in the Gospel, that they cannot be fully solved without the Gospel.

The problems being raised today – and is it really only today? – about human labour do not, in fact, come down in the last analysis – I say this with respect for all the specialists – either to technology or even to economics but to a fundamental category: the category of the dignity of work, that is to say, of the dignity of man. Economics, technology and the many other specializations and disciplines have their justification for existing in that single essential category. If they fail to draw from that category and are shaped without reference to the dignity of human labour, they are in error, they are harmful, they are against man.

This fundamental category is humanistic. I make bold to say that this fundamental category, the category of work as a measure of the dignity of man, is Christian. We find it in its highest degree of intensity in Christ.

Let this suffice, dear brothers. It was not on one occasion alone that I met you here as your Bishop and dealt more abundantly with all these themes. Today, as your guest, I must speak of them more concisely. But remember this one thing: Christ will never approve that man be considered, or that man consider himself, merely as a means of production, or that he be appreciated, esteemed and valued in accordance with that principle. Christ will never approve of it. For that reason he had himself put on the Cross, as if on the great threshold of man's spiritual history, to oppose any form of degradation of man, including degradation by work. Christ remains before our eyes on his Cross, in order that each human being may be aware of the strength that he has given him: 'he gave (them) power to become children of God' (Jn 1:12).

This must be remembered both by the worker and the employer, by the work system as well as by the system of remuneration; it must be remembered by the State, the nation, the Church.

When I was with you, I tried to give witness to this. Pray that I may continue to give that witness in the future also, all the more now that I am in Rome; pray that I may continue to give that witness before all the Church and before the modern world.

3. I am thinking with joy of the blessing of the magnificent church at Mistrzejowice, now that its building is well advanced. You all know that I remember the beginning of this work at Mistrzejowice, its very beginning; and all the stages of the building that followed. Together with you I go back

in prayer and heart to the tomb of Father Joseph, of holy memory, the priest who began this work, putting all his strength into it and sacrificing all his young life on its altar. I thank all those who are continuing this work with so much love and perseverance.

At this moment my thoughts go also to the Krzesławice Hills. The efforts of many years are slowly bearing fruit. With all my heart I bless this work and all the other churches rising or about to rise in this area and in the other constantly growing quarters.

From the Cross of Nowa Huta began the new evangelization, the evangelization of the second Millennium. This church is a witness and confirmation of it. It arose from a living awareness and responsible faith and must continue to serve that faith.

The evangelization of the new millennium must refer to the teaching of the Second Vatican Council. It must be, as that Council taught, a work shared by Bishops, priests, religious and laity, by parents and young people. The parish is not only a place where catechesis is given, it is also the living environment that must actualize it.

The church whose building you are bringing to a conclusion with so much effort but also with so much enthusiasm is rising in order that by its means the Gospel of Christ may enter into the whole of your lives. You have built the church; build your lives with the Gospel.

May Mary Queen of Poland and Blessed Maximilian Kolbe help you in this continually.

VISIT TO THE FAMILY TOMB AND TO THE BASILICA OF OUR LADY OF CRACOW

The visit was intended to be a private one. Instead it became a great, warm-hearted display of solidarity with and devotion to the Holy Father. During Saturday afternoon, John Paul II paid a visit to Cracow cemetery to pray at his family's tomb. The visit was not referred to in the official programme and, in order to prevent the crowds of faithful causing traffic jams in the city, the authorities requested the newspapers not to mention it. But it did not happen that way. In Cracow, the entire population was tuned in to the pilgrimage of Peter's successor.

By early afternoon, hundreds of the faithful were already crowding the neighbourhood of the cemetery. It was a demonstration of great maturity and solidarity. There was no applause when the Holy Father's car arrived at 4.30 p.m., or when the Pope walked towards the tomb and knelt beside it in prayer. Everybody prayed. They prayed in silent sympathy, united to the Pope in fervent spiritual emotion. It was only when the Holy Father left the cemetery that he was warmly applauded by all those present. And this applause, in the atmosphere of reflection which prevailed, seemed like a tangible expression of prayer.

The Pope's route to the Basilica of Our Lady of Cracow, *Kosciol Mariacki*, where he was to meet the nuns of the Archdiocese, was lined by expectant crowds as he drove past in an open car.

The meeting with the nuns also was not mentioned in the programme of the day's visits, but they turned out in large numbers for the Pope. The shrine of our Lady was filled to overflowing and they greeted him, as with a single voice, singing hymns to Our Lady and songs of welcome.

John Paul II, in a brief address, recalled how he daily received Vatican nuns from different religious orders for whom he celebrated Mass in his private chapel. He expressed the desire to live a life of harmony as did the Polish nuns and as happened also with the nuns in Rome. With frequent interruptions due to the singing of hymns, the Pope continued his simple and homely speech by saying that he knew well how devoted the nuns were to the Church, to St Peter and to his successor whoever he might be.

Turning to the image of the Madonna on the high altar of the Basilica, the Pope concluded his message by urging the nuns to love in the same way as the Madonna, whose outstretched hands were a sign of abundant grace. 'You should wish', said the Holy Father, 'that your hands might be outstretched to all the people.'

The meeting with the nuns of the Archdiocese ended at 6.45 p.m., but it was not until an hour later that the Pope reached his residence. The Holy Father's procession passed very slowly down the church and through the streets of the city to the Archbishop's house, as if weighed down by the constant tribute of affection which was manifested to him.

A MEETING WITH VISITING BISHOPS

During the afternoon, the Pope received,
in the audience chamber of the
Archbishop's Palace, a great number of
bishops from different countries and
other dioceses in Poland. The Pope
addressed these prelates as follows:

Venerable Brothers,
Gentlemen,

I am very happy to be able to have this meeting with you, the guests of the
Church in Poland, who have come from various countries to take part in the
solemn jubilee celebrations commemorating the ninth centenary of the
martyrdom of Saint Stanislaus of Szczepanów, the Bishop of Cracow. Once
again I would like to express my sincere thanks for your kindness in taking
part in these celebrations. You agreed to come when the venerable Primate of
Poland, Cardinal Stefan Wyszynski, and I myself, at that time the
Metropolitan Archbishop of Cracow, extended to you a cordial invitation.

1. These celebrations take on a special meaning and have a loud echo also
from the fact that, through a mysterious plan of Divine Providence, I was
called last October by the Cardinal Electors from the See of Saint Stanislaus to
the Chair of Saint Peter. At this time then it is my will to participate in this
solemn jubilee as a guest, joining the faithful of Poland and pilgrims from
the whole world in venerating the glorious figure of my saintly Predecessor in
the See of Cracow and in asking, at the beginning of my Pontificate, his
heavenly protection in carrying out my new worldwide pastoral service.

Stanislaus was born in the first half of the eleventh century in the town of
Szczepanów. Because of his deep piety and his cultural preparation he was
named a canon in the Cathedral of Bishop Lambert Zula. At the death of
Bishop Lambert, Pope Alexander II, at the request of the clergy and the lay
people as well as of King Boleslaus II himself, raised Stanislaus to the See of
Cracow. His episcopal ministry was very short, from 1072 to 1079, barely
seven years! But how intense it was, how, meritorious, how heroic!

History tells how the relationship between Bishop Stanislaus and King
Boleslaus II, serene at first, later deteriorated because of the injustices and
cruelty visited by the King upon his subjects. The Bishop of Cracow, an
authentic 'good shepherd' (cf. John 10:10–14), defended his flock. The King
replied with violence. Bishop Stanislaus was killed while celebrating Mass.
On the venerated skull of the Martyr, now preciously preserved in an artistic
reliquary, one can still see the signs of the heavy moral blows.

2. From that time on, Saint Stanislaus became the Patron of Poland. He
became especially the benefactor and protector of poor people; he became,
above all, an example to Bishops as to how to communicate and defend the
sacred deposit of faith with undaunted strength and unbending spirit. For

centuries he has been considered an illustrious witness to genuine freedom and to the fruitful synthesis which is brought about in a believer between loyalty to an earthly fatherland and fidelity to the Church, which lives in the expectation of a definitive and future city (cf. Heb 13:14).

Even after nine centuries the personality and the message of Saint Stanislaus preserve an extraordinary relevance. This regards both his life as a pastor of a portion of God's People and the witness of blood given by his martyrdom.

But Saint Stanislaus is certainly and especially 'the man' of his times: his pastoral ministry is fulfilled under the pontificate of Saint Gregory VII, in a period, that is, in which the Church claims her own freedom and her own original spiritual mission in the face of the powerful men of the world. In the eleventh century, Poland and the Church in Poland, at the beginning of the second century of their history, also found themselves in the sphere of complex and delicate problems, which at that time both Europe and Christianty itself had to live and face.

If the Polish Episcopate has decided to invite so many illustrious guests, it has done so in order to emphasize these historical bonds. And it is in the name of these bonds that I desire to thank you for your presence.

And hence, if on this extraordinary occasion I desire to wish something for everybody, it is that this our common meditation on the events which took place nine hundred years ago may help us to see with even greater clarity the mission of Christianity and of the Church in their relationship to the modern world. Perhaps this has a particular importance for the Europe of today that finds herself at a point of new searching for her distinctive and suitable path.

The task of Christianity and of the Church cannot be anything other than a creative participation in these efforts. Only in this way, and in no other, can there be expressed and actuated our solicitude for the preservation and defence of the Christian patrimony of Europe and of the individual European countries.

With these hopes I renew my sentiments of deep gratitude and I ask for you an outpouring of heavenly blessings. As a sign of my esteem and regard, I impart to you my Apostolic Blessing.

. . . that apostolic gesture of
the imposition of hands

Sunday 10 June

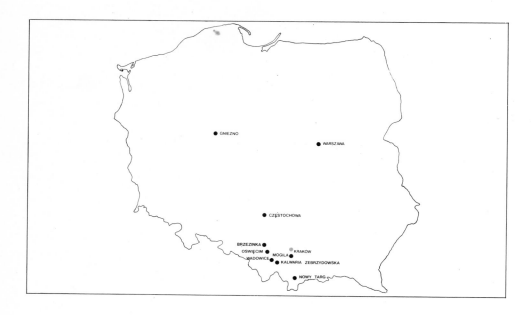

THE PONTIFICAL HIGH MASS IN
HONOUR OF ST STANISLAUS AT
CRACOW

On the great meadow in the centre of
Cracow called *Błonia Krakowskie*, there
were gathered on Sunday 10 June
some three million of the faithful to take
part in the Mass at which John Paul II
officiated.
It was the solemn conclusion of two
events of historical importance for the
universal Church – the jubilee of St
Stanislaus and the pilgrimage of the
Holy Father in Poland. During the Mass,
in which many bishops from all parts of
the world took part, John Paul II
delivered the following sermon:

Praised be Jesus Christ!

1.   Today all of us gathered here together find ourselves before a great mystery in the history of the human race: Christ, after his Resurrection met the Apostles in Galilee and spoke to them the words which we have just now heard from the lips of the deacon who proclaimed the Gospel: 'Full authority has been given to me both in heaven and on earth; go, therefore, and make disciples of all the nations. Baptize them in the name of the Father, and of the Son, and of the Holy Spirit. Teach them to carry out everything I have commanded you. And know that I am with you always, until the end of the world' (Mt 28:18–20).

These words contain a great mystery in the history of humanity and in the history of the individual human person.

Every person goes forward. He or she goes forward towards the future. Nations also go forward. So does all humanity. To go forward, however, does not only mean to endure the exigencies of time, continuously leaving behind the past: yesterday, the years, the centuries. To go forward also means being aware of the goal.

Could it be perhaps that the human person and humanity itself journey only through this world and then disappear? Could it be perhaps that everything for a human being consists only in what is built, conquered, and enjoyed in this world? Beyond the conquests and the totality of life here (culture, civilization, technology) is there nothing else awaiting a human person? 'The form of this world is passing away.' Is the human person going to pass away along with it?

The words that Christ spoke in his farewell to the Apostles express the mystery of human history, the history of each person and of all persons, the mystery of the history of humanity.

Baptism in the name of the Father and of the Son and of the Holy Spirit is an immersion into the living God, into 'Him who is' as the Book of Genesis puts it; into 'Him who was, who is, and who will be' according to the Book of Revelation (1:4). Baptism is the beginning of an encounter, of a unity, of a communion for which earthly life is merely a preface, an introduction. The fulfilment and completion belong to eternity. 'The form of this world is passing away.' Therefore we must find the 'world of God' to arrive at our destination, to find fulfilment in life and in the human vocation.

Christ has shown us the way and, in his farewell to his Apostles, he has reconfirmed this once more. He told them and the whole Church to teach and carry out all that he commanded: 'And know that I am with you always, until the end of the world.'

2.   We always listen to these words with the greatest emotion. They were spoken by the risen Redeemer to delineate the history of humanity and at the

same time the history of each human person. When he says 'make disciples of all nations,' we see before our mind's eye the moment when the Gospel was first brought to our nation, the beginnings of its history when the first Poles were baptized in the name of the Father and of the Son and of the Holy Spirit. The spiritual profile of the history of our motherland is traced out by these very words of Christ spoken to the Apostles. The spiritual profile of the history of each one of us is also traced out in about the same way.

A human person is a free and reasonable being. He or she is a knowing and responsible subject. He or she can and must, with the power of personal thought, come to know the truth. He or she can and must choose and decide. That Baptism, which was received at the beginning of Poland's history, makes us more conscious of the authentic greatness of the human person. 'Immersion into water' is a sign of being called to participate in the life of the Most Blessed Trinity. At the same time it is an irreplaceable affirmation of the dignity of every human person. The very fact of the call itself already testifies to this. If he or she is called to such a participation, the human person must possess an exceptional dignity.

Likewise the whole historical process of a person's knowledge and choices is closely bound up with the living tradition of his or her own country where, down through all generations, the words of Christ echo and resound along with the witness of the Gospel, Christian culture, and the customs that derive from faith, hope and charity. A human being makes his choices with knowledge and with interior freedom. Here tradition is not a limiting factor but a treasure, a spiritual enrichment. It is a great common good which is confirmed by every choice, by every noble deed, by every life authentically viewed as Christian.

Can one cast all this off? Can one say no? Can one refuse Christ and all that he has brought into human history?

Certainly not. It is true that man is free. But the basic question remains: is it licit to do this? In whose name is this licit? By virtue of what rational argument, what value close to one's will and heart would it be possible to stand before yourself, your neighbour, your fellow-citizens, your country, in order to cast off, to say no to all that we have seen for one thousand years? To all that has created and always constituted the basis of our identity?

One time Christ asked the Apostles (this took place after the promise of the institution of the Eucharist and many left him): 'Do you too wish to go away?' (Jn 6:67). Allow the Successor of Peter, before all of you gathered here together, before all of our history, before modern society to repeat today the words of Peter, which constituted his reply to the question of Christ: 'Lord, to whom shall we go? You have the words of eternal life' (Jn 6:68)!

3. Saint Stanislaus was, as historical sources confirm, the Bishop of Cracow for seven years. This Bishop, a fellow-citizen of ours, born in Szczepanow not far away from here, assumed the See of Cracow in 1072. He left it in 1079,

suffering death at the hands of Boleslaus the Bold. The day of his death, the sources say, was 11 April and this is the day on which the liturgical calendar of the universal Church commemorates Saint Stanislaus. In Poland the solemnity of this Bishop Martyr has been celebrated for centuries on 8 May and it continues thus even now.

When I, as the Metropolitan of Cracow, began with you to prepare for the ninth centenary of the death of Saint Stanislaus, which occurs this year, we all were still under the influence of the one thousandth anniversary of the Baptism of Poland which was celebrated in the year of our Lord 1966. Under the influence of this event and remembering the figure of Saint Adalbert, who also was a Bishop and a martyr, whose life was connected in our history with the epoch of our Baptism, the figure of Saint Stanislaus seems to point (by analogy) to another sacrament, which is part of the Christian's initiation into the faith and into the life of the Church. This is the sacrament, as is well known, of the anointing or Confirmation. All of the jubilee studies of the mission of Saint Stanislaus in our thousand years of Christian history and all the spiritual preparation for this year's celebrations have reference to this sacrament of Confirmation.

This analogy has many aspects. Above all it parallels the normal development of a Christian life. Just as a baptized person comes to Christian maturity by means of this sacrament of Confirmation, so Divine Providence gave to our nation, after its Baptism, the historical moment of Confirmation. Saint Stanislaus, who was separated by almost a whole century from the period of the Baptism and from the mission of Saint Adalbert, especially symbolizes this moment by the fact that he rendered witness to Christ by his own blood. In the life of each Christian, usually a young Christian because it is in youth that one receives this sacrament – and Poland too was then a young nation, a young country – the sacrament of Confirmation must make him or her become a 'witness to Christ' according to the measure of one's own life and proper vocation. This is a sacrament which is especially associated with the mission of the Apostles inasmuch as it introduces every baptized person into the apostolate of the Church (especially into the so-called apostolate of the laity).

This is the sacrament which brings to birth within us a sharp sense of responsibility for the Church, for the Gospel, for the cause of Christ in the souls of human beings, and for the salvation of the world.

The sacrament of Confirmation is received by us only once in our lifetime (just as Baptism is received only once). All of life which opens up in view of this sacrament assumes the aspects of a great and fundamental test: a test of faith and of character. Saint Stanislaus has become, in the spiritual history of the Polish people, the patron of this great and fundamental test of faith and of character. In this sense we honour him also as the patron of the Christian moral order. In the final analysis the moral order is built up by means of human beings. This order consists of a large number of tests, each one a test of faith and of character. From every victorious test the moral order is built up. From every failed test moral disorder grows.

We know very well from our entire history that we must not permit, absolutely and at whatever cost, this disorder. For this we have already paid a bitter price many times.

This is therefore our meditation on the seven years of Saint Stanislaus, on his pastoral ministry in the See of Cracow, on the new examination of his relics, that is to say his skull, which still shows the marks of his moral wounds — all of this leads us today to a great and ardent prayer for the victory of the moral order in this difficult epoch of our history.

This is the essential conclusion of all the hard work for this centennial, the principal condition and purpose of conciliar renewal for which the Synod of the Archdiocese of Cracow has so patiently worked, and also it is the main prerequisite for all pastoral work, for all the activity of the Church, for all tasks, for all duties and programmes which are being or will be undertaken in the land of Poland.

That this year of Saint Stanislaus would be a year of special historical maturity in our nation and in the Church in Poland, a year of a new and knowledgeable responsibility for the future of our country and of the Church in Poland — this is the vow that I desire today, here with you my venerable and dear brothers and sisters, to make, as the first Pope of Polish stock, to the Immortal King of the ages, the Eternal Shepherd of our souls and of our history, the Good Shepherd!

4.   Allow me now to sum up by embracing spiritually the whole of my pilgrimage to Poland, from its beginning on the eve of Pentecost at Warsaw to its conclusion today at Cracow on the solemnity of the Most Holy Trinity. I wish to thank you, dear fellow-countrymen, for everything. For having invited me and for having accompanied me along the whole course of the pilgrimage, through Gniezno of the Primates and through Jasna Góra. I thank again the State authorities for their kind invitation and their welcome. I thank the Authorities of the Provinces of Poznań. Częstochowa, Nowy Sacz and Bielsko, as well as the Municipal Authorities of Warsaw and — for this final stage — the Municipal Authorities of the ancient royal City of Cracow, for all that they have done to make possible my stay and pilgrimage in Poland. I thank the Church in my homeland: the Episcopate, with the Cardinal Primate at its head, the Metropolitan of Cracow and my beloved brother Bishops, Julian, Jan Stanisław and Albin, with whom it was granted to me to work for many years in preparing the Jubilee of Saint Stanislaus. I thank the whole of the Clergy. I thank the religious orders of men and women. I thank you all and each one in particular. It is our duty and salvation, always and everywhere to give thanks.

I too wish now, on this last day of my pilgrimage through Poland, to open my heart wide and to speak aloud my thanks in the magnificent form of a Preface. How great is my desire that my thanksgiving will reach the Divine Majesty, the heart of the Most Holy Trinity: the Father and the Son and the Holy Spirit!

My fellow-countrymen, with the greatest warmth I again give thanks, together with you, for the gift of having been baptized more than a thousand years ago in the name of the Father and of the Son and of the Holy Spirit, the gift of having been immersed in the water which, through grace, perfects in us the image of the living God, in the water that is a ripple of eternity: 'a spring of water welling up to eternal life' (Jn 4:14). I give thanks because we human beings, we Poles, each of whom was born as a human being of the flesh (cf. Jn 3:6) and blood of his parents, have been conceived and born of the Spirit (cf. Jn 3:5). Of the Holy Spirit.

Today, then, as I stand here in these broad meadows of Cracow and turn my gaze towards Wawel and Skalka, where nine hundred years ago 'the renowned Bishop Stanislaus underwent death', I wish to fulfil again what is done in the sacrament of Confirmation, the sacrament that he symbolizes in our history. I wish what has been conceived and born of the Holy Spirit to be confirmed anew through the Cross and Resurrection of our Lord Jesus Christ, in which our fellow-countryman Saint Stanislaus shared in a special way.

Allow me, therefore, like the Bishop at Confirmation, to repeat today the apostolic gesture of the laying on of hands. For it expresses the acceptation and transmission of the Holy Spirit, whom the Apostles rectified from Christ himself after his Resurrection, when, 'the doors being shut' (Jn 20:19), he came and said to them: 'Receive the Holy Spirit' (Jn 20:22).

This Spirit, the Spirit of salvation, of redemption, of conversion and holiness, the Spirit of truth, of love and of fortitude, the Spirit inherited from the Apostles as a living power, was time after time transmitted by the hands of the bishops to entire generations in the land of Poland. This Spirit, whom the Bishop that came from Szczepanow transmitted to the people of his time, I today wish to transmit to you, as I embrace with all my heart yet with deep humility the great 'Confirmation of history' that you are living.

I repeat therefore the words of Christ himself:
'Receive the Holy Spirit' (Jn 20:22).
I repeat the words of the Apostle:
'Do not quench the Spirit' (1 Thess 5:19).
I repeat the words of the Apostle:
'Do not grieve the Holy Spirit' (Eph 4:30).

You must be strong, dear brothers and sisters. You must be strong with the strength that comes from faith. You must be strong with the strength of faith. You must be faithful. Today more than in any other age you need this strength. You must be strong with the strength of hope, hope that brings the perfect joy of life and does not allow us to grieve the Holy Spirit.

You must be strong with love, which is stronger than death. You must be strong with the love that 'is patient and kind; . . . is not jealous or boastful; . . . is not arrogant or rude . . . does not insist on its own way; . . . is not irritable or resentful; . . . does not rejoice at wrong, but rejoices in the right . . . bears all things, believes all things, hopes all things, endures all things. Love never ends' (1 Cor 13:4–8).

You must be strong with the strength of faith, hope and charity, a charity that is aware, mature and responsible and helps us to set up the great dialogue with man and the world rooted in the dialogue with God himself, with the Father through the Son in the Holy Spirit, the dialogue of salvation.

That dialogue continues to be what we are called to by all 'the signs of the times'. John XXIII and Paul VI, together with the Second Vatican Council, accepted this call to dialogue. John Paul II confirms this same readiness from the first day of his pontificate. Yes, we must work for peace and reconciliation between the people and the nations of the whole world. We must try to come closer to one another. We must open the frontiers. When we are strong with the Spirit of God, we are also strong with faith in man, strong with faith, hope and charity which are inseparable, and ready to give witness to the cause of man before the person who really has this cause at heart. The person to whom this cause is sacred. The person who wishes to serve this cause with his best will. There is therefore no need for fear. We must open the frontiers. There is no imperialism in the Church, only service. There is only the death of Christ on Calvary. There is the activity of the Holy Spirit, the fruit of that death, the Holy Spirit who is always with all of us, with the whole of mankind, 'until the end of the world' (Mt 28:20).

5.   Again, there is in Warsaw, on Victory Square, the tomb of the Unknown Soldier, where I began my pilgrim ministry in the land of Poland; and here in Cracow on the Vistula, between Wawel and Skalka, there is the tomb of 'the Unknown Bishop' of whom a marvellous 'relic' is preserved in the treasure house of our history.

And so, before I leave you, I wish to give one more look at Cracow, this Cracow in which every stone and every brick is dear to me. And I look once more on my Poland.

So, before going away, I beg you once again to accept the whole of the spiritual legacy which goes by the name of 'Poland,' with the faith, hope and charity that Christ poured into us at our holy Baptism.

I beg you
— never lose your trust, do not be defeated, do not be discouraged;
— do not on your own cut yourselves off from the roots from which we had our origins.

I beg you
— have trust and notwithstanding all your weakness, always seek spiritual power from him from whom countless generations of our fathers and mothers have found it.
— never detach yourself from him.
— never lose your spiritual freedom, with which 'he makes a human being free'.

— do not disdain charity, which is 'the greatest of these' and which shows itself through the Cross. Without it human life has no roots and no meaning.

All this I beg of you

174

— recalling the powerful intercession of the Mother of God at Jasna Góra and at all her other shrines in Polish territory.

— in memory of Saint Adalbert who underwent death for Christ near the Baltic Sea.

— in memory of Saint Stanislaus who fell beneath the royal sword at Skalka.

— all this I beg of you.

Amen.

THE MEETING WITH JOURNALISTS AND OTHERS EMPLOYED IN THE MASS MEDIA

Before returning to Rome from Cracow, John Paul II held a meeting in the Convent of the Franciscans for all the journalists and other representatives of the mass media who had covered his journey in Poland. To them he spoke as follows:

Dear friends,

I have already met you before a long way from here, but even though the Successor of Peter is able to feel at home in any part of the globe — seeing that his mandate is for the sake of 'all nations' (Mt 28:19) — it is nevertheless a source of particular satisfaction and pleasure for me to welcome you here, in my native land. My prayer is that in the shrines and sacred places where the Polish people have expressed their faith with such intensity you yourselves may derive great enrichment of spirit and profound inner peace.

The pilgrimage is a practice that has a long tradition among us Christians.

Some places are regarded as particularly sacred on account of the holiness and acquired virtue of certain people who lived in them; their sacredness increases with the passage of time through the prayers and sacrifices of the multitudes of pilgrims who come to visit them.

Thus virtue begets more virtue, grace attracts grace, and the goodness of a holy man or woman, kept perennially alive in the memory of an entire people, continues to cast its light across the centuries, bringing renewal, inspiration and healing to successive generations. In this way we are helped and encouraged in the difficult uphill pursuit of virtue.

You may remember that one of the first things I wanted to do, almost as soon as I became Pope, was to go on a pilgrimage to the shrines of the national patrons of Italy, Saint Francis of Assisi and Saint Catherine of Siena. I felt then the need to assure myself of the help of these great saints and to seek at their shrines the resolution and counsel my formidable new task required. But I also felt the profound need to strengthen my spirit by making a pilgrimage to the holy places of my own country, and I thank God that in his goodness he has enabled me to do so and made it possible precisely during this year when Poland is celebrating the ninth centenary of the death of her principal patron, Saint Stanislaus.

And now, at the moment of my departure, I thank you, my friends in the mass media, for being with me during my pilgrimage. I thank you and the various communications agencies that you represent for having brought the entire world — as I think I can say you have — to Poland, keeping it by my side and enabling it to share with me these precious days of prayer and my own homecoming.

As I express to you my profound gratitude I would like to ask of you one more favour. I would like to ask you to tell the world and the people of your own countries that Pope John Paul II remembered them, held them close to his heart, and prayed for them at every stage of his pilgrimage: at the shrines of the Holy Mother of God in Warsaw, Częstochowa, Nowy Targ and Maków; by the tombs of Saint Wojciech and Saint Stanislaus in Gniezno and Cracow; at the shrine of the Holy Cross in Mogiła and in the cells of Auschwitz, where Blessed Maximilian Kolbe spent the last heroic hours of his life. Tell them — for it is true — that the Pope prays for them every day and many times a day, wherever he finds himself, and asks them to pray for him. And now a special word for you who exercise your profession through the press, the photographic agencies, radio, television and the cinema. Each day, as I watch you at work, I am increasingly struck by the nobility of the task that has been entrusted to you through your vocation and profession.

I have already said on a previous occasion (Mexico, January 1979) that by disseminating information that is 'complete, accurate, exact and faithful', you make it possible for each man or woman to be aware of and responsible for the 'general progress of all' (*Communio et progressio* 34–19). Ideally your lives are devoted to the service of the truth. Only by remaining faithful to this ideal will you merit the respect and gratitude of your fellow men.

In this connection, I would like to remind you of what Jesus Christ said during the trial that was to decide his fate — and this was his unique contribution to his own defence: 'For this I was born and for this I have come into the world, to bear witness to the truth' (Jn 18:37).

Apply it to your own lives, and each of you will find that it is able to calm your sorrows and strengthen your courage in most of the trials and frustrations of your existence.

This is the thought I would leave you with until we meet again. Take back my greetings and my thanks to your families and my special love to your children. As I say goodbye to you and to Poland, I give you my heartfelt blessing.

THE FAREWELL AT THE AIRPORT OF BALICE

John Paul II ended his pilgrimage in Poland at the airport of Balice. Before boarding the aircraft, the Pope addressed a farewell message to all those who were present.

Mr Chairman of the Council of State of the Polish People's Republic! Gentlemen!

1.   The time has come for me to take my leave of Cracow and of Poland.

Although it can in no way break the profound spiritual and emotional ties that bind me to my city, to my native land and to its citizens, just now I feel this separation painfully. However, Rome is now my episcopal See and it is necessary that I return there: to Rome, where no son of the Church, and indeed we might say no man, be he a Pole or a member of some other nation, is a stranger.

Now is the moment for farewells and thanks, and I wish in the first place to address my words of thanks to the Chairman of the Council of State, who, together with the other representatives of the government, has come here to say goodbye to me, just as nine days ago he welcomed me to my native land in the name of the leaders of the Polish Republic.

I thank him for this double act of courtesy which I so greatly appreciated and always will appreciate on account of what it signifies.

I wish, furthermore, here in this place, to express my heartfelt thanks for the hospitality extended to me, to which the State authorities too, central and local, contributed so much. And I would particularly say thank you once more for the meeting at the Belvedere, on the first day of my visit to Poland.

I hope that this visit, which is now drawing to a close, will contribute to the further development of relations between Church and State in Poland, as well as between Poland and the Holy See.

I fully realize what a wealth of delicacy the word 'hospitality' signifies, but at the same time I appreciate, in this case, the effort it implies, the number of problems it conceals within it, the work that went into the preparations, the decisions that had to be made, and finally the effort that went into its realization.

And so to all I say 'thank you', and I wish this 'thank you' to reach all to whom my thanks are due — and I don't know that there is anyone in Poland to whom I am not a debtor in this respect.

I believe I should thank everyone. I address the tokens of my gratitude to the government authorities, to the authorities in the individual provinces, and to the authorities in the city of Cracow.

2.   Most worthy Cardinal Primate of Poland, I extend my warmest thanks to you also for the words of farewell which you spoke in your own name and on behalf of the entire Polish Church. I sought to respond to your words of welcome with the service which, thanks to divine Providence and to your own goodwill, I have been able to render during the past few days. Now it simply remains to me with all my heart to thank Your Eminence, the Episcopate, priests, religious families of men and women, and all the People of God in Poland for the warm and heartfelt sentiments and for the prayers which have gone with me throughout this unforgettable pilgrimage from Warsaw, through the Gniezno of Saint Adalbert and Jasna Góra, to Saint Stanislaus in Cracow. I thank God for your faith, and for your loyalty to the Holy See and to the Successor of Peter.

My short stay in Poland has merely served to strengthen my spiritual ties with my beloved country and with the Church from which I come and which I wish to serve with all my heart and with all my strength through my universal mission as Pope.

I thank you for having assured me a remembrance in your prayers. There, beyond the Alps, I will listen in spirit to the sound of the bells which call the faithful to prayer, above all to the *Angelus*, and at the same time I will hear the heartbeat of my countrymen.

3.   The visit of the Pope to Poland is certainly an unprecedented event, not only for this century but also for the entire Millennium of Christian life in Poland — especially as it is the visit of a Polish Pope, who has the sacrosanct right to share the sentiments of his own nation. Such a sharing, in fact, is an integral part of his ministry to the whole Church as the Successor of Peter.

This unprecedented event is undoubtedly an act of courage, both on the part of those who gave the invitation and on the part of the person who was invited. However, in our times, such an act of courage is necessary. It is necessary to have the courage to walk in the direction in which no-one has walked before, just as once Simon needed the courage to journey from the lake of Gennesaret in Galilee towards Rome, a place unknown to him.

Our times have great need of an act of witness openly expressing the desire to bring nations and regimes closer together, as an indispensable condition for peace in the world. Our times demand that we should not lock ourselves into the rigid boundaries of systems, but seek all that is necessary for the good of man, who must find everywhere the awareness and certainty of his authentic citizenship. I would have liked to say: the awareness and certainty of his pre-eminence in whatever system of relations and powers.

Thank you, then, for this visit, and I hope that it will prove useful and that in the future it will serve the aims and values that it had intended to accomplish.

magnificent witness of the history of the nation and of the Church that it is now; I express the wish that the cultural heritage enclosed within its walls may continue to speak with its unique contents.

I take leave of Poland! I take leave of my native land! As I depart I kiss the ground, from which my heart can never be detached.

May Almighty God bless you: the Father, the Son, and the Holy Spirit.

AT THE AIRPORT OF CIAMPINO

It was 7.25 p.m. on Sunday 10 June
when the Pope's aircraft touched down
at Ciampino Airport near Rome. John
Paul II made the following speech to the
authorities and to a crowd of the
faithful who had gone to the airport to
welcome the pilgrim Pope on his return
from Poland:

Mr President of the Council of Ministers,

Please accept my grateful appreciation for the noble words with which you
have welcomed me on my return to Italy, in your own name and on behalf of
the Government and the whole nation.

The Pope has visited his native land, the place in which he came to the
light of day and the light of faith, where he consecrated himself to Christ and
the Church, and now he returns to his See, where the Lord has placed him to
guide and confirm his brethren, to Rome, the city chosen by providence to be
the dwelling-place of the Vicar of Christ himself. I thank God for having
been able to see Poland again, that blessed and fertile land in which I put
down my roots as a man, as a priest and as a bishop, drawing from it rich
and life-giving nourishment. I thank him with great fervour for having
brought me back here, where my spirit wishes to make its home and become
daily more identified with the universal mission entrusted to me. One
motherland, my native one, has prepared me and sent me back to the other
one, the larger one, the Catholic one, which embraces as does my service, the
whole world.

I am happy to be able to express at this moment the profound happiness
in my heart at having been able to take part in the centenary celebrations of
the martyrdom of Saint Stanislaus. Warsaw, Gniezno, Czestochowa and
Cracow, the stopping-places of my pilgrimage, have been moments of joyous
communion, friendship, constructive talks and especially of prayer. The deep
and intimate emotions of the various meetings have blended together in my
soul, and have enriched it with a new and gratifying experience that is a pure
grace of the Most High.

Before my eyes I have the recollected, peaceful and praying crowds of
brothers and sisters, sons and daughters, my fellow-countrymen, who have
wished to make their tribute of devoted affection to him who is a son of the
same country, but above all the visible Head of the Church, the
Successor of Peter. The faith of Poland is a living and vibrant reality, a reality
which I would like to enable you to share in; like all genuine expressions of
faith, it contains a message of optimism and hope: 'Christ . . . having been
raised from the dead will never die again. Death has no more power over him'
(Rom 6:9). This secure affirmation of Saint Paul, with which I ended my
greeting to the Polish faithful in the Cathedral in Warsaw, I now pass on to
you, and through you to beloved Rome and to Italy, as a message of salvation
that finds ever new confirmation in ourselves, in society and in the fellowship

of peoples, provided that faith in Christ inspires our responsible choices.

At the conclusion of my journey, I am glad to renew my good wishes and greetings to the whole Polish Nation, the Polish Episcopate, led by Cardinal Stefan Wyszynski, Primate of Poland, and to send a renewed expression of cordial thanks to the Representatives of the Authorities of the State for the consideration and attentiveness with which they welcomed and surrounded me.

I would assure you that before the venerated picture of Our Lady of Czestochowa I said a very special prayer for the destiny of Italy, and for the well-being, peaceful coexistence and serene prosperity of her citizens; in telling you this I wish to extend to all here present a respectful and cordial greeting, and I also express my lively gratitude: to the Cardinals; to the Italian civil and military Authorities, who with their deferential and spontaneous welcome have made my hour of return even happier; to the distinguished members of the Diplomatic Corps, whose presence witnesses to the sharing of their various nations in the joy of my pilgrimage; to all of you who with your festive welcome have made me the gift of a genuine family atmosphere; to the personnel of the Aviation Company, and to all who have contributed to the excellent organization of the journey, making it both comfortable and attractive. For all of you the assurance of my affection and benevolence is signified by my Blessing, which I extend to the Eternal City and to the whole Catholic world.

Diary of Events